Table of Contents

Parent Tips 2	Vowel Pairs: *er*, *ir*, and *ur* 80
Beginning and Ending Letter Sounds 4	Vowel Pairs: *ar* and *or* 82
Short and Long Vowels 12	Vowel Pairs: *ai* and *ay* 84
Missing Short Vowels 14	Vowel Pairs: *oi* and *oy* 86
Short Vowels Review 19	Vowel Pairs: *au* and *aw* 88
Missing Long Vowels 22	Vowel Pairs: *ou* and *ow* 90
Long Vowels Review 27	Vowel Pairs: *ee* and *ea* 92
Y as Long *i* Sound 32	Vowel Pairs: *oa* and *ow* 94
Y as Long *e* Sound 33	Vowel Pairs: Short *oo* and Long *oo* 96
Y as Long *i* and Long *e* Sound 34	Vowel Pairs: *ew* and *iu* 98
Short and Long Vowels Review 36	Vowel Pairs Review 100
Consonant Blends 41	Word Families 104
Consonant Blends with *s* 42	More Activities 128
Consonant Blends with *r* 48	Phonics Practice Menu 129
Consonant Blends with *l* 54	Rainbow Word Family 130
Consonant Blends Review 60	Word Search 131
Hard *c* and Soft *c* Sounds 62	Tounge Twisters 132
Hard *g* and Soft *c* Sounds 66	A Web About... 133
Final Consonant Blends: *st* and *sk* 70	Practice Page 134
Final Consonant Blends: *nd*, *nk*, and *nt* 72	How am I Doing 135
Word with *sh* and *ch* 74	Reading Strategies 136
Words with *th* and *wh* 76	Answers 138
Silent Letters 78	Certificate 160

© Chalkboard Publishing Inc Canadian Phonics 2

Parent Tips

Set Realistic, Suitable Goals

At the start of each week, motivate your child to take ownership of their learning by having them set one or two goals. Then develop a shortlist of activities, exercises, and tasks to accomplish those goals. Be sure the activities are appropriate, and those agreed-upon goals are realistic.

Establish a Consistent Study Place and Time

Set aside 20 minutes, preferably around the same time each day. This will help your child to develop a routine.

Designate a Quiet Study Space

Make sure the study space is well lit and free from big distractions such as a television. Try to keep interruptions to a minimum by keeping cell phone ringers off.

Provide Necessary Learning Tools

Be ready for learning by having writing tools, art supplies, and paper at your child's fingertips.

Come Up With a Fun Name

Come up with a positive name for working on skills, such as "Brain Stretch Time," "Brain Booster," or "Brain Aerobics." By doing so, your child will view it as something beneficial and fun.

Give Effective Praise

Give specific praise for your child's efforts and the process. By giving genuine praise and constructive feedback about their performance and efforts, you're teaching your child to tie their successes with the strategies and steps they're developing. This will ultimately encourage your child to see themselves as capable and confident learners.

Here are some examples!

I like the way you...
I noticed that you...
Tell me how you...

thought
used
explored
created
decided
chose

Always focus on their progress!

Instead of "Good job!"
Try "I like the way you kept trying even when you were frustrated"
Try "I like the way you check your work!"

Encouraging a Growth Mindset

The research of psychologist Dr. Carol Dweck tells us that people have two possible mindsets—a fixed mindset or a growth mindset. People with a fixed mindset believe that they are either smart or good at something, or they are not—and nothing can change that. People with a growth mindset believe that it is always possible to get better at doing something. Dr. Dweck has found that children with a growth mindset are more motivated to learn and achieve more than children with a fixed mindset.

How can you help children develop a growth mindset?

Talk about the brain: Explain that the brain becomes stronger by working hard to master new skills. Just as exercise makes muscles stronger, working at challenging thinking tasks makes the brain stronger.

View mistakes as learning opportunities: Let your child know that mistakes are valuable ways of learning where the problems lie. By carefully looking at mistakes, you and your child can learn where there are misunderstandings or missing pieces of knowledge. Mistakes pave the way to success!

Teach ways of dealing with frustration: Children can "turn off" when they become frustrated, which makes learning impossible. Teach your child ways to overcome frustration. For example, use the Internet to learn about breathing techniques that combat stress. You can also remind your child of skills that they have mastered in the past (such as learning to tie shoelaces) that took time and effort to learn.

Focus on praising the process: While it's fine to praise your child or the results they achieved, you can encourage a growth mindset by focusing your praise on the process. For example, praise your child's willingness to keep trying and their use of effective learning strategies, such as asking questions.

Model a growth mindset: Look for opportunities to reinforce with your child how to see things from a growth mindset. For example:

If your child says...	Respond by saying...
I'll never get this!	Maybe you can't do it yet, but you'll get better if you keep trying.
I've been working at this for a long time and I'm still not getting it right!	Look at these areas where you've made progress. Keep working and you'll make more progress.
Hey, I can finally do this!	Let's think about how you achieved success. Some of the things you did this time might help you with the next challenge.

Beginning and Ending Sounds Review

Beginning Letter Sounds

Say the name of the object out loud.
Print the letter that is the beginning sound for the object's name.

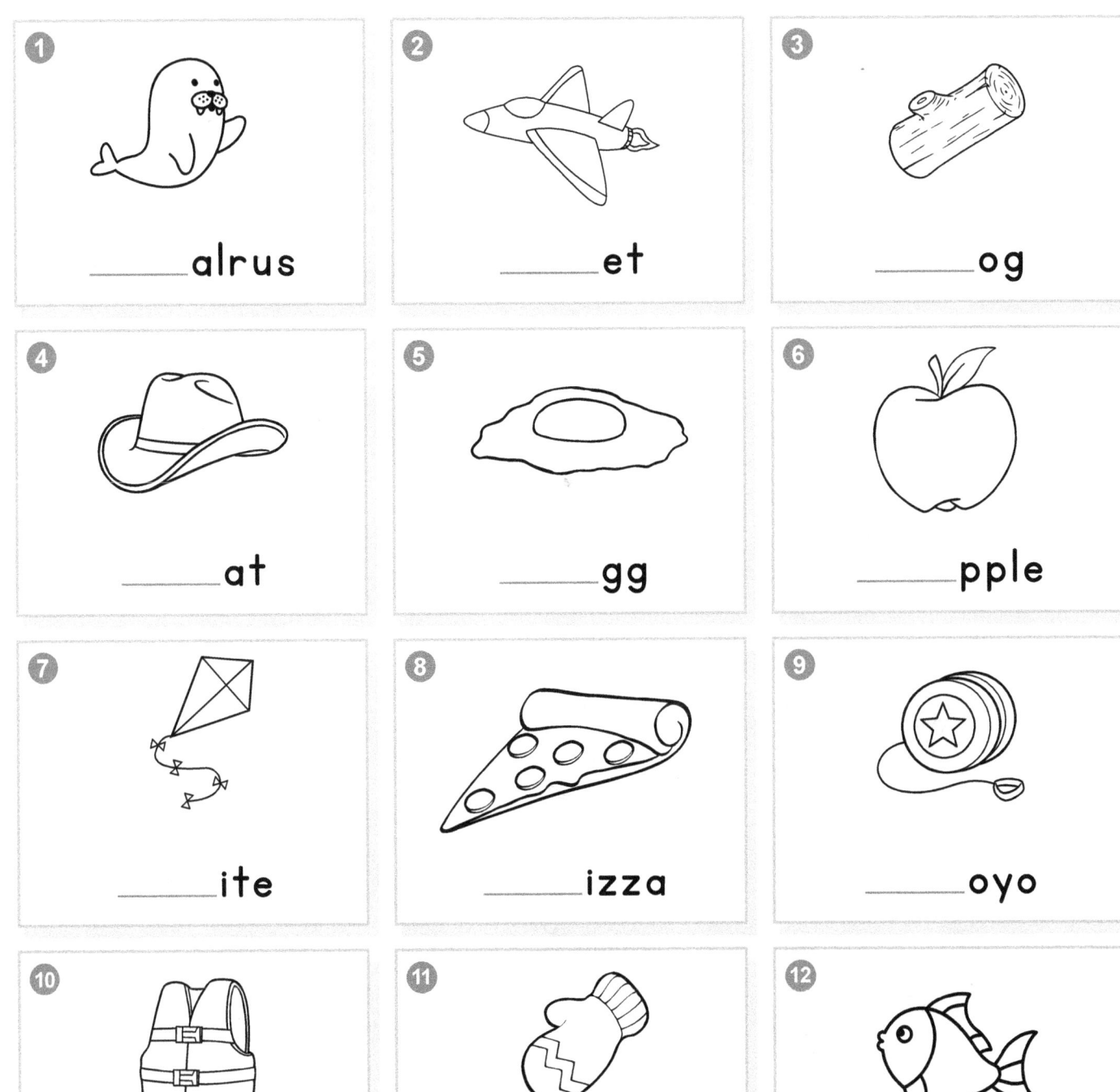

1. ___alrus
2. ___et
3. ___og
4. ___at
5. ___gg
6. ___pple
7. ___ite
8. ___izza
9. ___oyo
10. ___est
11. ___itten
12. ___ish

Beginning Letter Sounds

Say the name of the object out loud.
Print the letter that is the beginning sound for the object's name.

1. ___ wl
2. ___ ap
3. ___ et
4. ___ agon
5. ___ ctopus
6. ___ ipper
7. ___ uilt
8. ___ uice
9. ___ ork
10. ___ ree
11. ___ oon
12. ___ ainbow

Ending Letter Sounds

Say the name of the object out loud.
Circle the ending sound for the object's name.

Ending Letter Sounds

Say the name of the object out loud. Colour in the ending sound for the object's name.

1.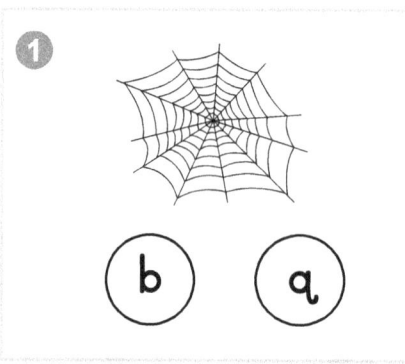
   (b) (q)

2.
   (m) (d)

3.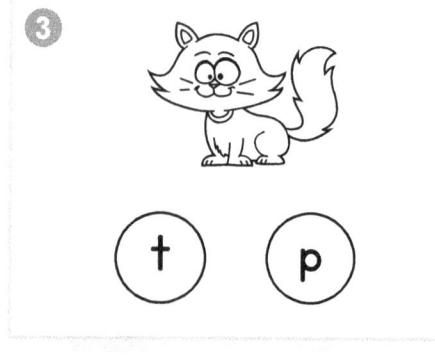
   (t) (p)

4.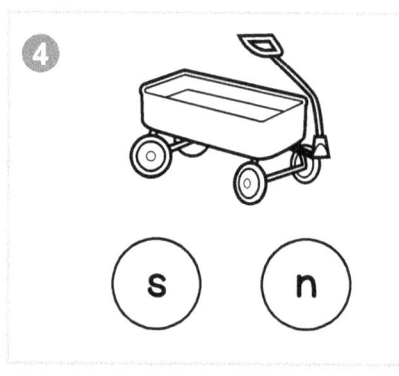
   (s) (n)

5.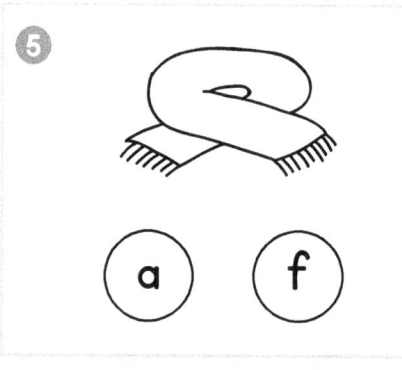
   (a) (f)

6.
   (a) (g)

7.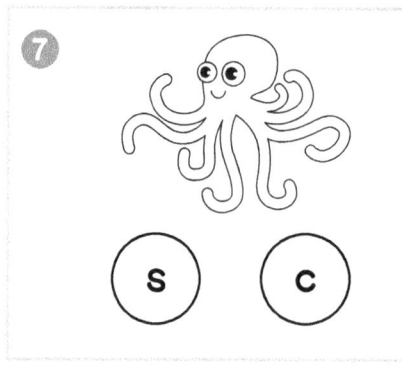
   (s) (c)

8.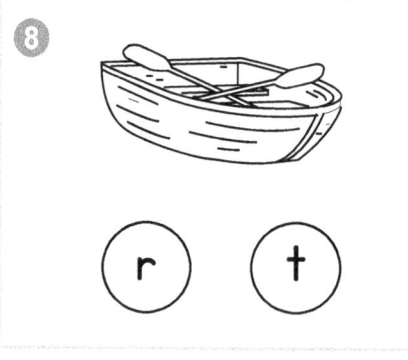
   (r) (t)

9.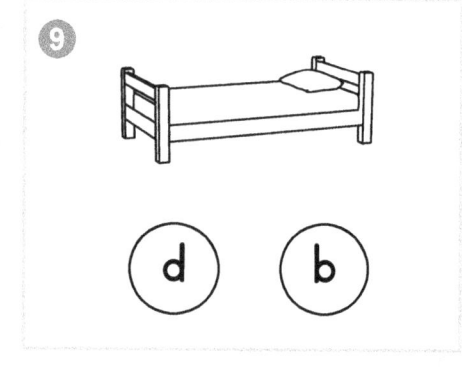
   (d) (b)

10.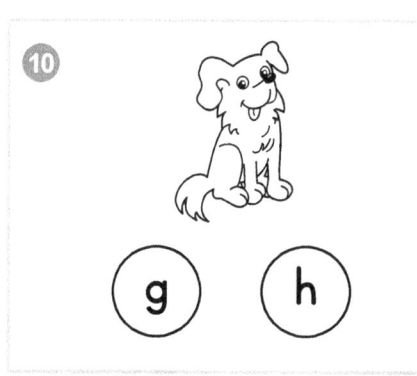
    (g) (h)

11.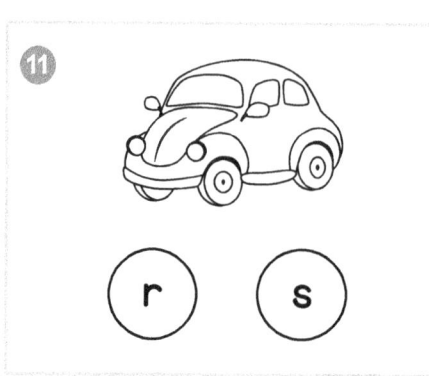
    (r) (s)

12.
    (k) (j)

Beginning and Ending Letter Sounds

Say the name of the object out loud. Print the letters that are the beginning sound and ending sound for the object's name.

Beginning and Ending Letter Sounds

Say the name of the object out loud. Print the letters that are the beginning sound and ending sound for the object's name.

Beginning and Ending Letter Sounds

Say the name of the object out loud. Print the letters that are the beginning sound and ending sound for the object's name.

1.  __ o l __

2.  __ a l a __

3.  __ e a __

4.  __ i l __

5.  __ e m o __

6. 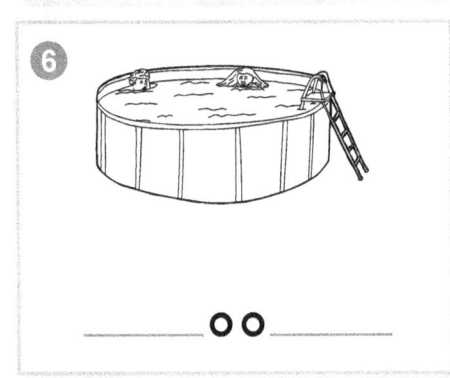 __ o o __

7.  __ a r __

8. 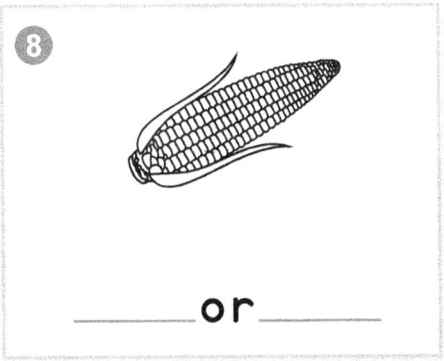 __ o r __

9.  __ o a __

10.  __ a n __

11. 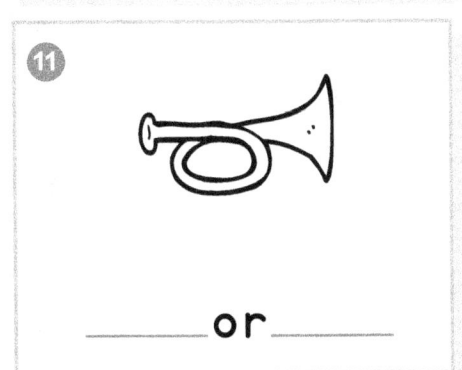 __ o r __

12.  __ u l __

© Chalkboard Publishing Inc

Short and Long Vowels

Short and Long Vowels

Long vowels say their name. Short vowels make different sounds. Read the examples below. Say the names of the objects out loud.

Missing Short Vowels

Say the name of the object out loud. Listen for the short vowel sound. Fill in the missing vowel. Colour the pictures.

①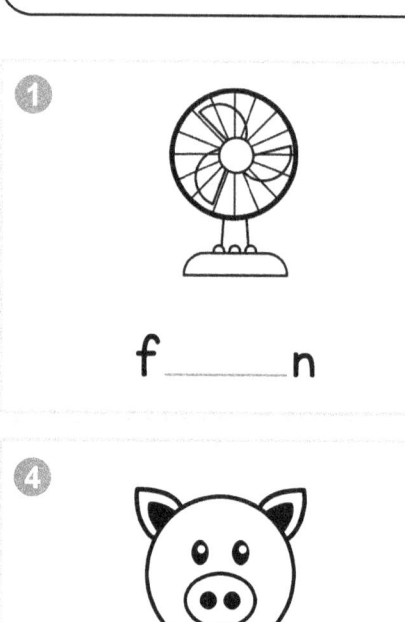
f____n

②
f____n

③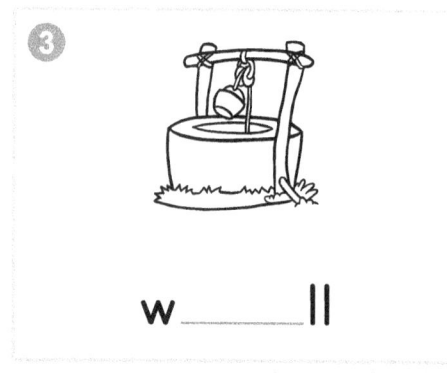
w____ll

④
p____g

⑤
j____m

⑥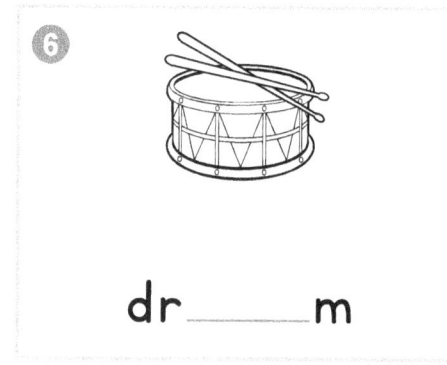
dr____m

⑦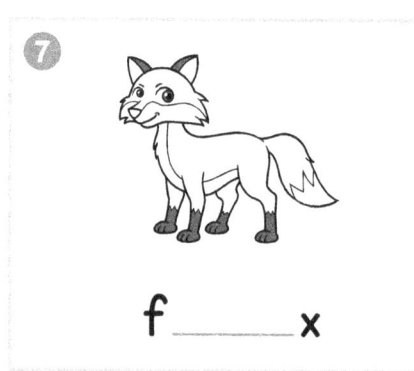
f____x

⑧
k____d

⑨
p____n

⑩
b____t

⑪
h____n

⑫
f____sh

Missing Short Vowels

Say the name of the object out loud. Listen for the short vowel sound. Fill in the missing vowel. Colour the pictures.

①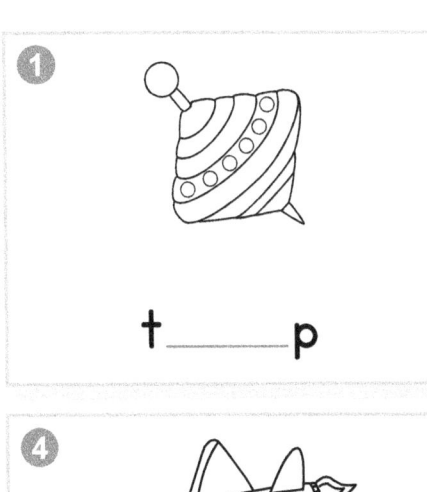
t___p

②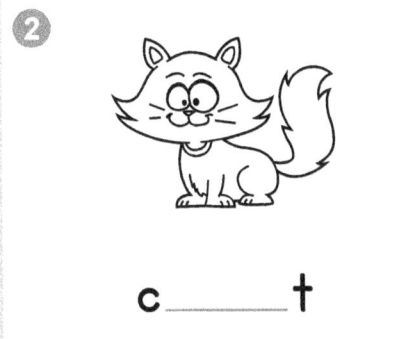
c___t

③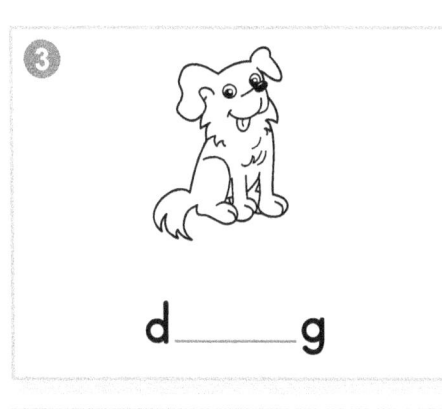
d___g

④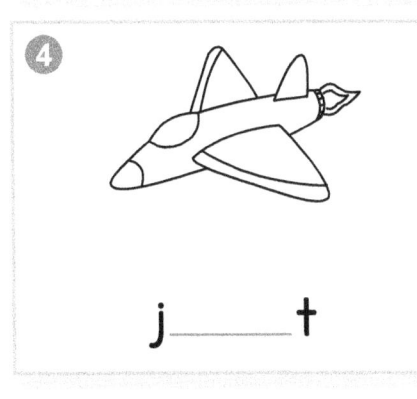
j___t

⑤
b___g

⑥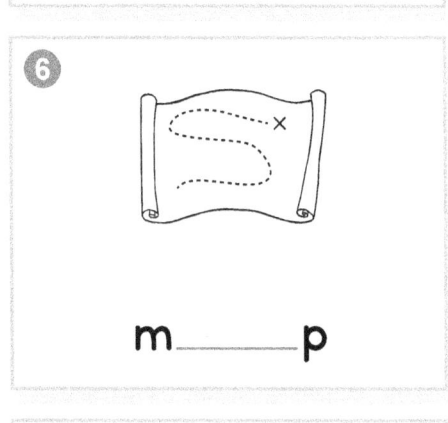
m___p

⑦
c___p

⑧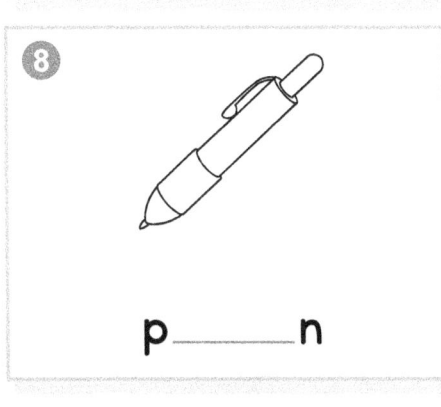
p___n

⑨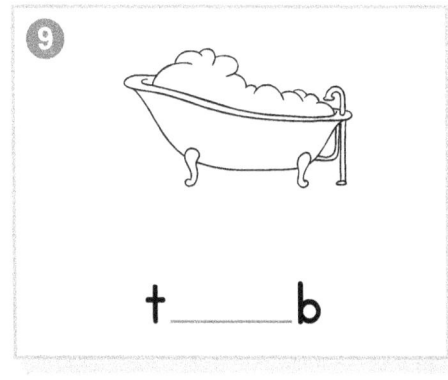
t___b

⑩
m___tten

⑪
d___ck

⑫
m___lk

Missing Short Vowels

Say the name of the object out loud. Listen for the short vowel sound. Fill in the missing vowel. Colour the pictures.

Missing Short Vowels

Say the name of the object out loud. Listen for the short vowel sound. Fill in the missing vowel. Colour the pictures.

1.
fr___g

2.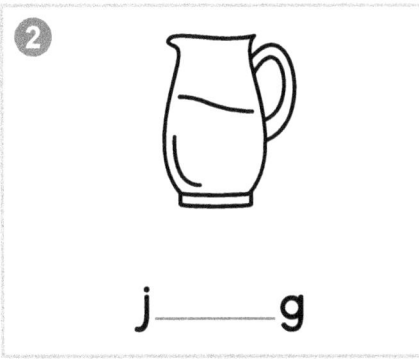
j___g

3.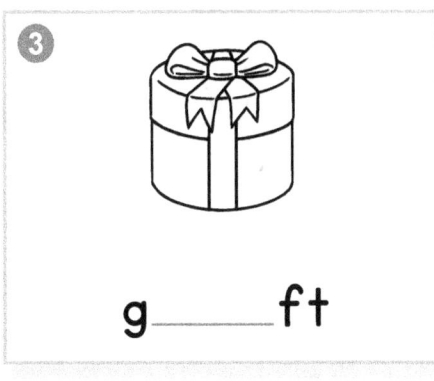
g___ft

4.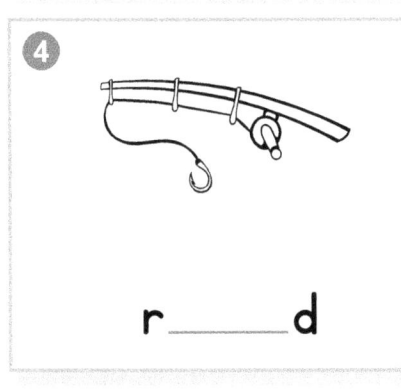
r___d

5.
s___n

6.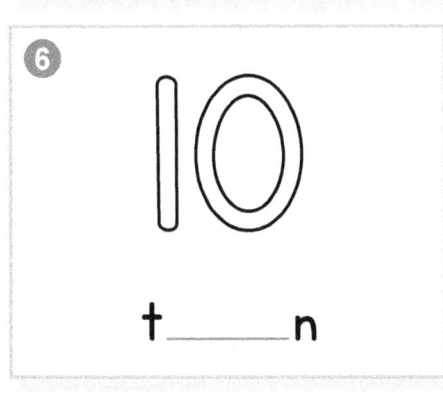
t___n

7.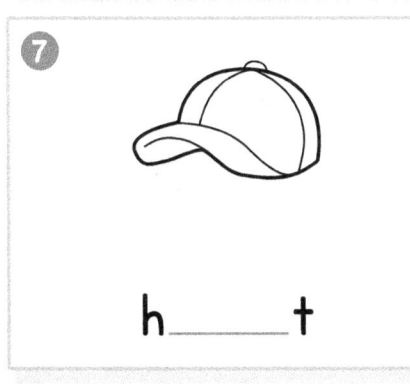
h___t

8.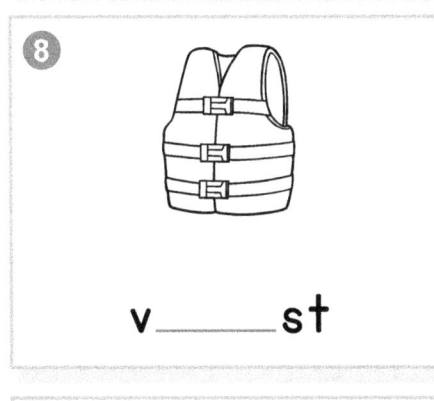
v___st

9.
h___g

10.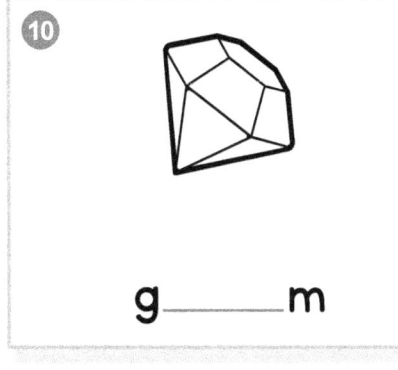
g___m

11.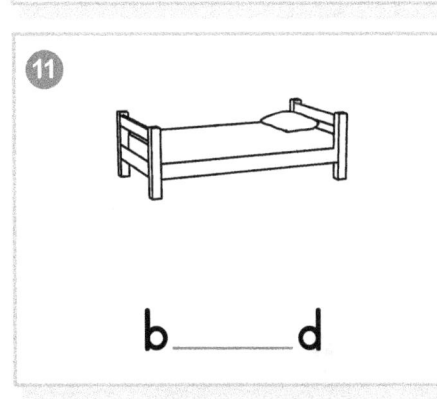
b___d

12.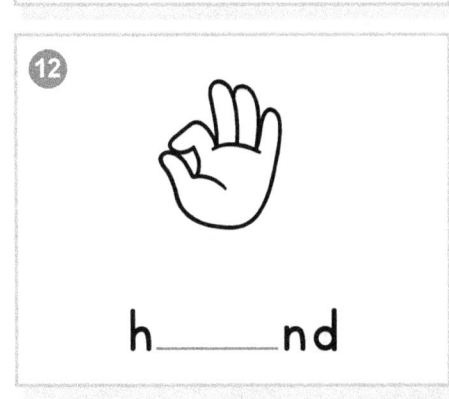
h___nd

Missing Short Vowels

Say the name of the object out loud. Listen for the short vowel sound. Fill in the missing vowel. Colour the pictures.

①
n___st

②
d___ll

③
s___x

④
p___t

⑤
n___t

⑥
r___t

⑦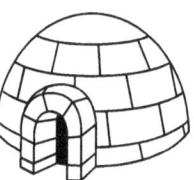
___gloo

⑧
m___p

⑨
b___s

⑩
b___x

⑪
b___g

⑫
___gg

© Chalkboard Publishing Inc

Short Vowel Review

Say the name of the object out loud.
Find the word. Look across for the word. Circle the word.

bug dog hut igloo jam king pan rod vest well

s	d	o	g	a	c	b	u	g
j	a	m	v	b	n	j	k	h
l	t	w	r	n	p	a	n	m
k	i	n	g	q	f	h	u	t
x	a	z	i	g	l	o	o	e
a	h	v	e	s	t	d	u	r
g	r	o	d	s	h	t	w	s
v	p	y	i	j	w	e	l	l

Short Vowel Review

Say the name of the object out loud.
Draw a line from the object to the matching word.

tub

log

sun

egg

bag

gift

cat

hen

top

pin

Short Vowel Review

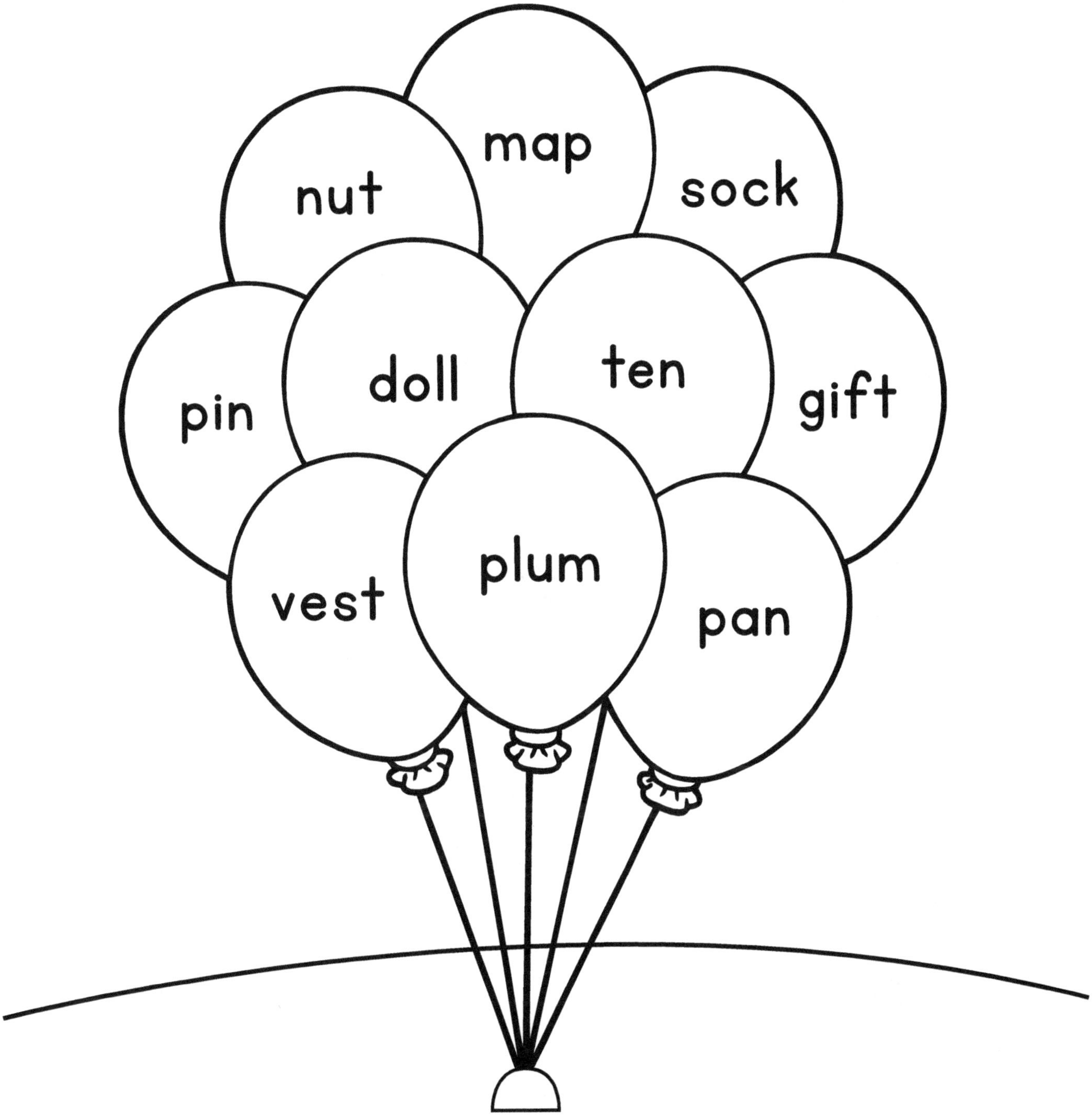

- nut
- map
- sock
- pin
- doll
- ten
- gift
- vest
- plum
- pan

Colour the ă words. — red
Colour the ĕ words. — blue
Colour the ĭ words. — green
Colour the ŏ words. — yellow
Colour the ŭ words. — purple

Missing Long Vowels

Say the name of the object out loud. Listen for the long vowel sound. Fill in the missing vowel. Colour the pictures.

1. c__ke
2. c__te
3. __ar
4. gl__be
5. m__al
6. m__le
7. __pe
8. f__el
9. J__ne
10. b__ne
11. l__af
12. s__al

Missing Long Vowels

Say the name of the object out loud. Listen for the long vowel sound. Fill in the missing vowel. Colour the pictures.

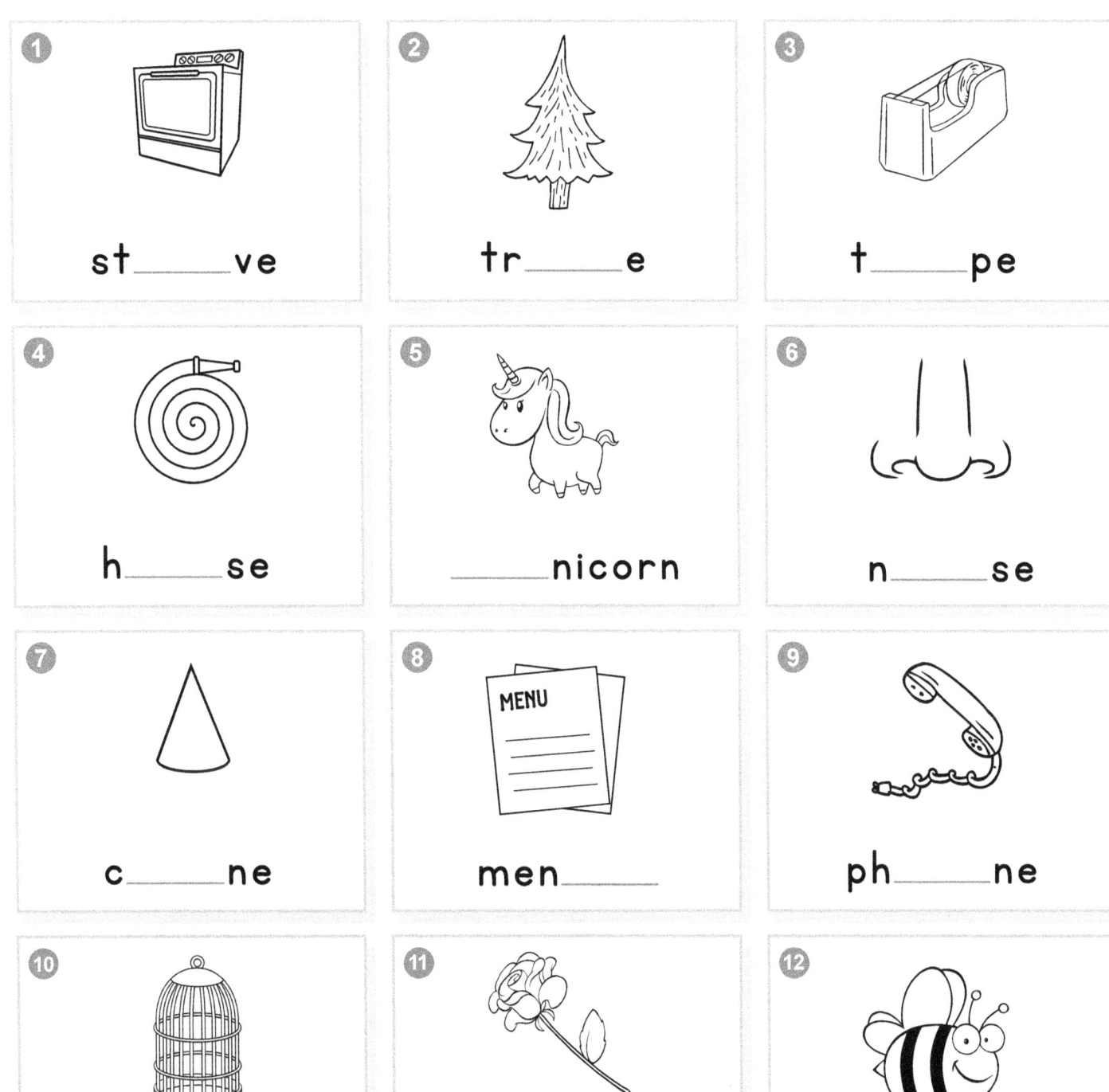

1. st__ve
2. tr__e
3. t__pe
4. h__se
5. __nicorn
6. n__se
7. c__ne
8. men__
9. ph__ne
10. c__ge
11. r__se
12. b__e

Missing Long Vowels

Say the name of the object out loud. Listen for the long vowel sound. Fill in the missing vowel. Colour the pictures.

1.
d____ce

2.
n____ne

3.
h____man

4.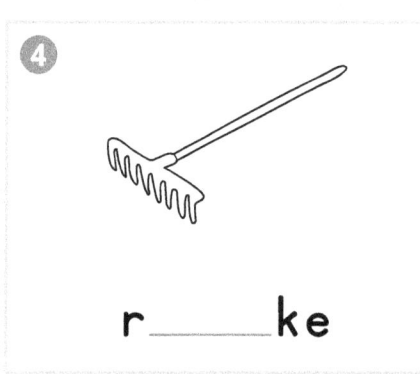
r____ke

5.
g____at

6.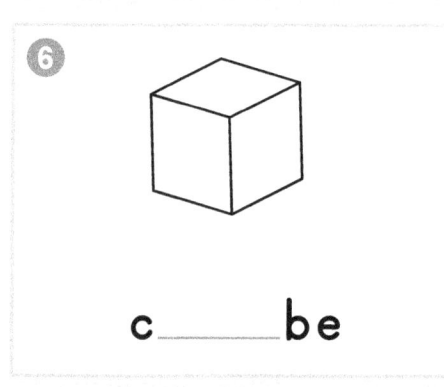
c____be

7.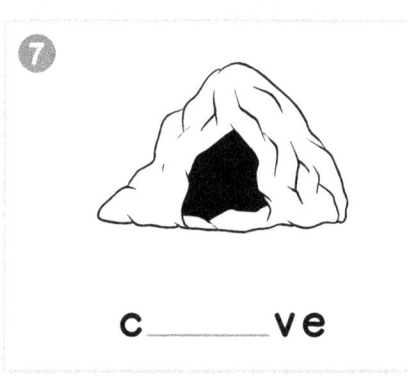
c____ve

8.
b____ak

9.
t____re

10.
sh____ep

11.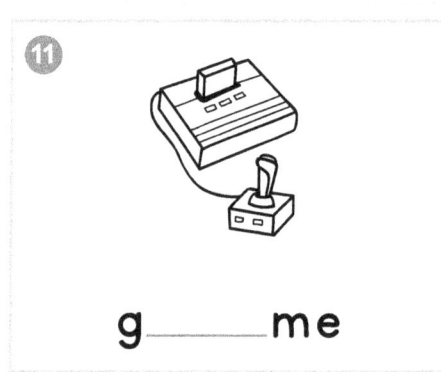
g____me

12.
n____te

Missing Long Vowels

Say the name of the object out loud. Listen for the long vowel sound. Fill in the missing vowel. Colour the pictures.

①
sl___de

②
r___be

③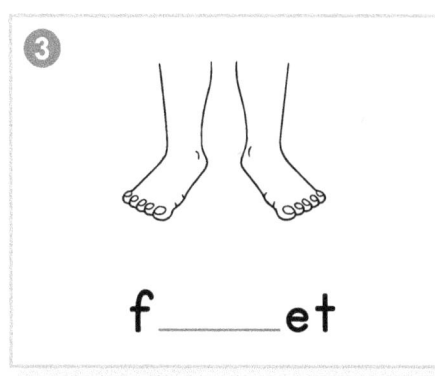
f___et

④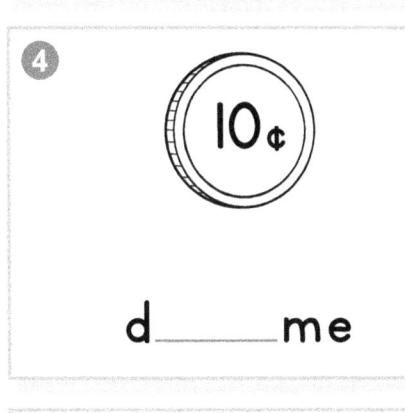
d___me

⑤
d___er

⑥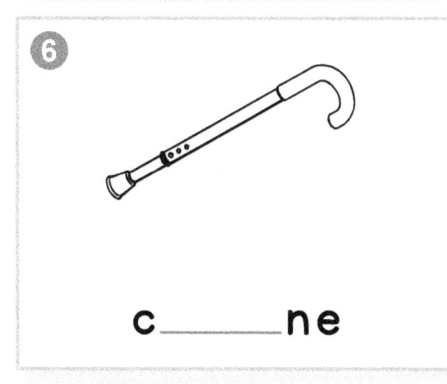
c___ne

⑦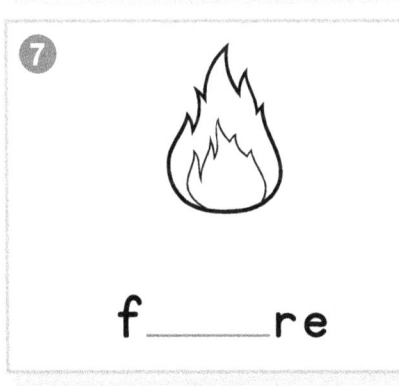
f___re

⑧
resc___e

⑨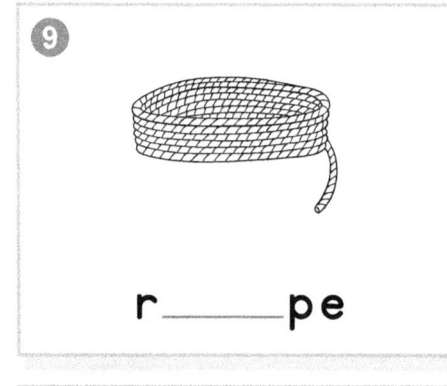
r___pe

⑩
m___ne

⑪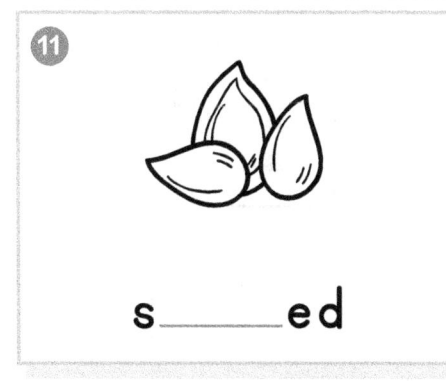
s___ed

⑫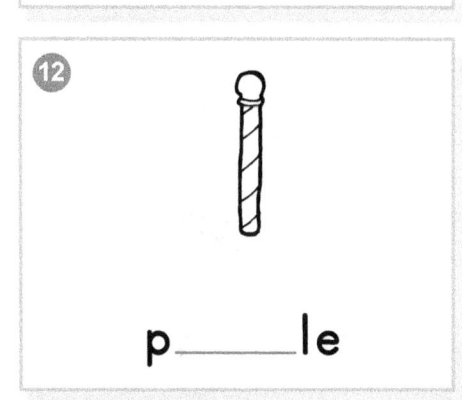
p___le

Missing Long Vowels

Say the name of the object out loud. Listen for the long vowel sound. Fill in the missing vowel. Colour the pictures.

①
r____eds

②
br____de

③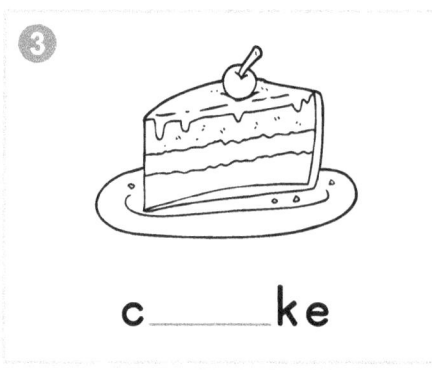
c____ke

④
pl____te

⑤
____nicycle

⑥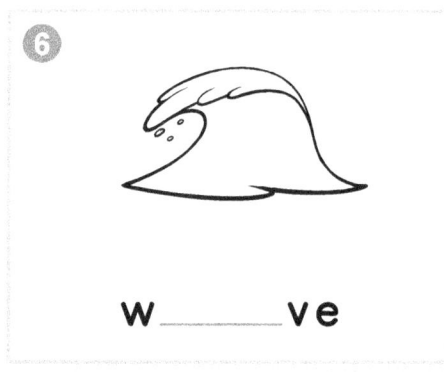
w____ve

⑦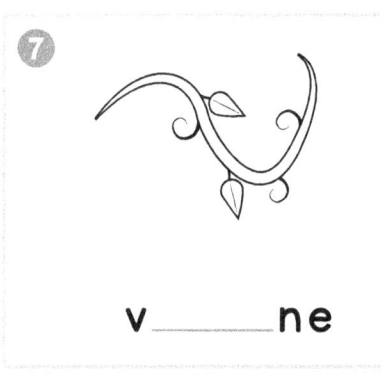
v____ne

⑧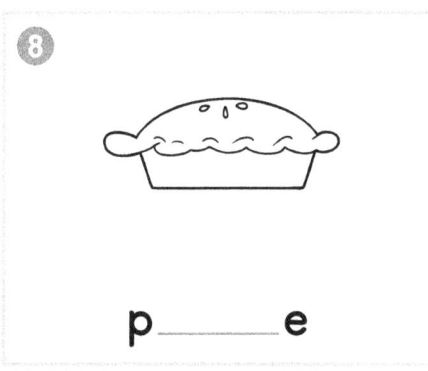
p____e

⑨
j____ice

⑩
h____ve

⑪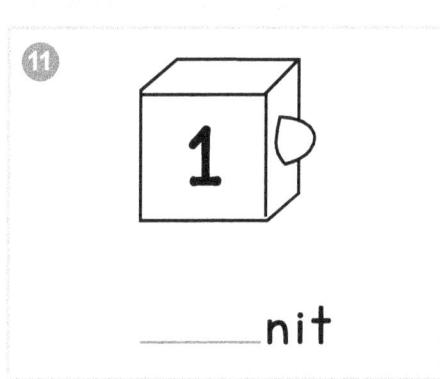
____nit

⑫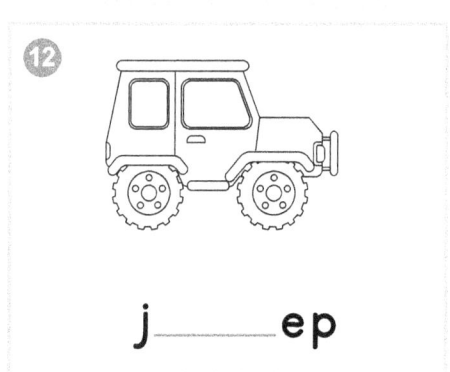
j____ep

Long Vowels Review

Say the name of the object out loud.
Find the word. Look across for the word. Circle the word.

  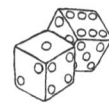       

cake   cute   dice   ear   game   phone   stove   tire   tree   unicorn

e	a	r	w	s	t	i	r	e
w	c	a	k	e	d	h	k	o
g	a	m	e	p	d	i	c	e
z	f	d	x	s	t	o	v	e
p	h	o	n	e	j	h	r	q
q	r	t	c	u	t	e	i	u
c	u	n	i	c	o	r	n	r
a	v	h	j	e	t	r	e	e

© Chalkboard Publishing Inc

Long Vowels Review

Say the name of the object out loud.
Draw a line from the object to the matching word.

leaf

June

globe

slide

plate

ice

ape

seal

hose

fuel

Long Vowels Review

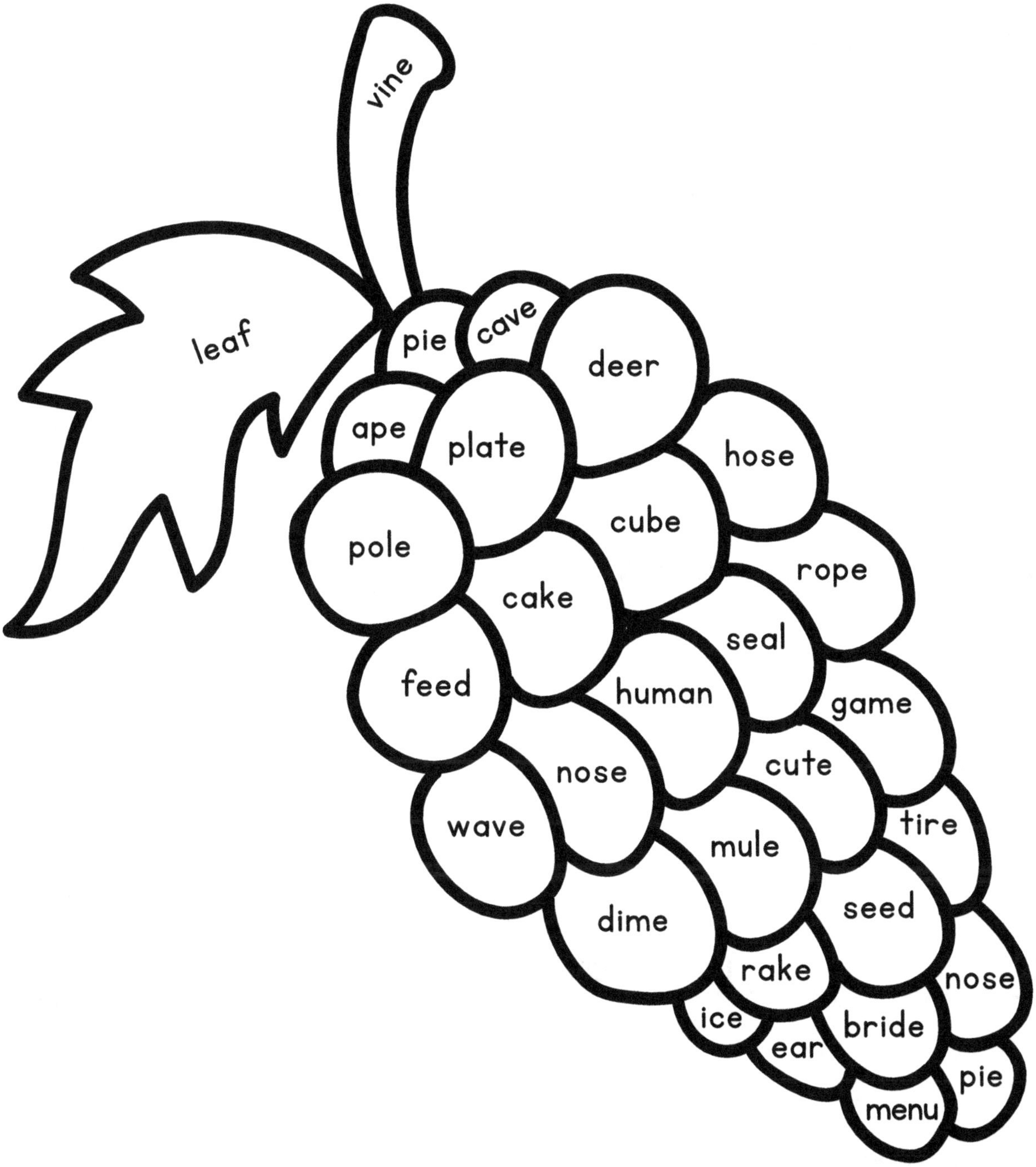
vine
leaf
pie
cave
deer
ape
plate
hose
pole
cube
rope
cake
seal
feed
human
game
nose
cute
wave
tire
mule
seed
dime
rake
nose
ice
ear
bride
pie
menu

Colour the $\bar{a}$ words. red

Colour the $\bar{e}$ words. blue

Colour the $\bar{\imath}$ words. green

Colour the $\bar{o}$ words. yellow

Colour the $\bar{u}$ words. purple

© Chalkboard Publishing Inc

Long Vowels Review

Read the sentence and say the name of the object out loud. Fill in the blank with the missing long vowel word.

cube   fire   game   gate   note   sheep

1

The _____ has six sides.

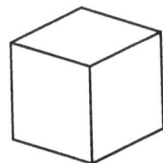

2

The _____ is warm and bright.

3

I left my friend a _____.

4

The _____ is lots of fun.

5

There is a shy _____ over there.

6

I close the _____ behind me.

Long Vowels Review

Read the sentence and say the name of the object out loud. Fill in the blank with the missing long vowel word.

bike   bone   cube   mane   meal   toes

1 I have five _____ on each foot.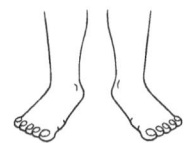

2 The pony has a shiny _____.

3 I ride my _____ to school.

4 The _____ is starting to melt.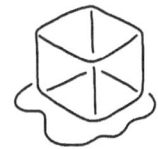

5 The dog likes to chew on a _____.

6 I ate the _____ and it was very tasty.

Y as Long i Sound

Sometimes the letter y makes a long *i* sound. Colour the pictures.

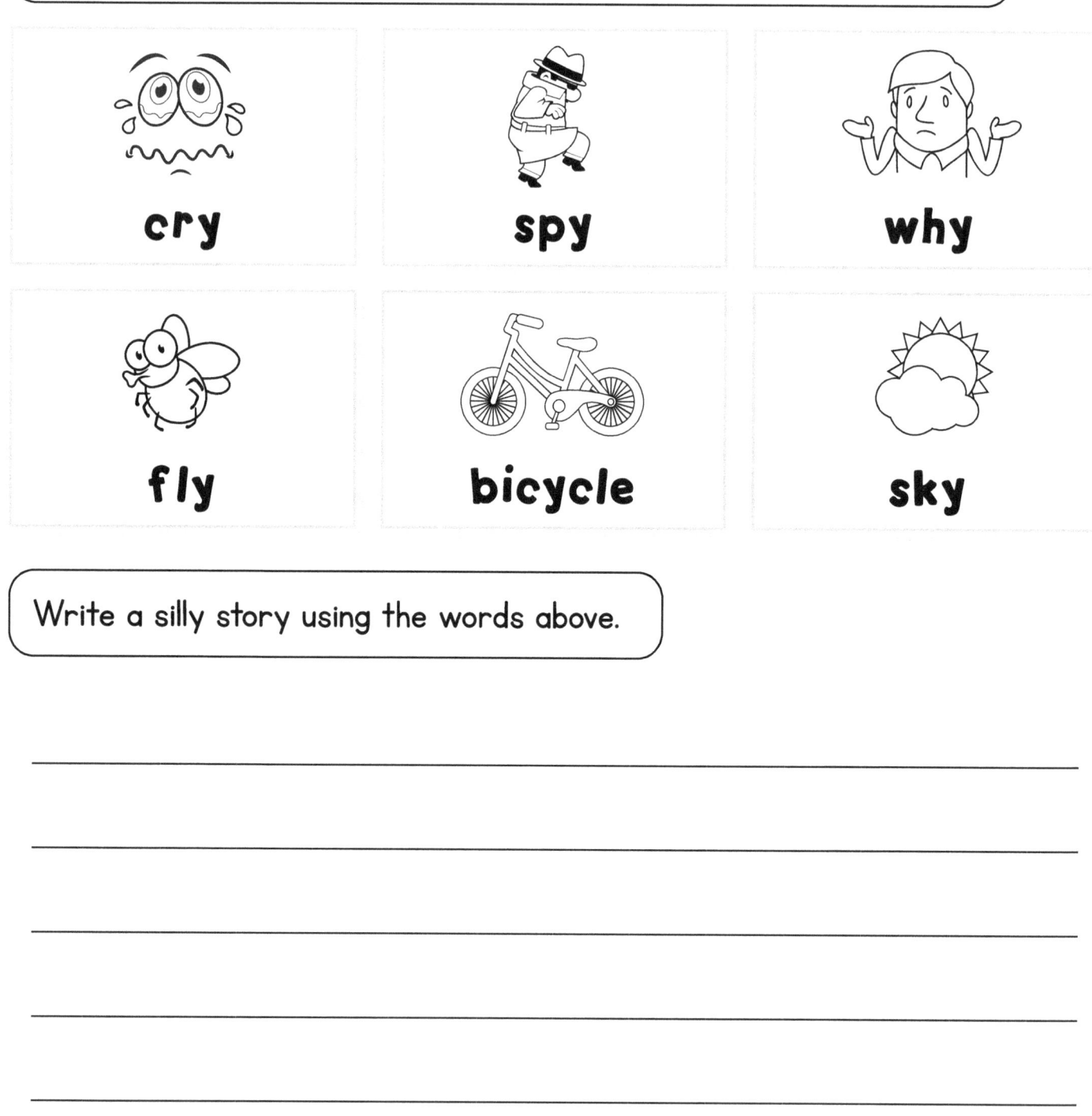

Write a silly story using the words above.

_____
_____
_____
_____
_____
_____

☐ I used capitals and end marks.   ☐ My printing is neat.   ☐ My writing makes sense.

Y as Long e Sound

Sometimes the letter *y* makes a long *e* sound. Colour the pictures.

| candy | cherry | bunny |
| ladybug | baby | jelly |

Write a silly story using the words above.

_____

_____

_____

_____

_____

☐ I used capitals and end marks.   ☐ My printing is neat.   ☐ My writing makes sense.

Y as Long i and Long e

Each word below has one of the two y sounds.
Circle the correct answer for each word.

1
Long ē
Long ī

2
Long ē
Long ī

3
Long ē
Long ī

4
Long ē
Long ī

5
Long ē
Long ī

6
Long ē
Long ī

7
Long ē
Long ī

8
Long ē
Long ī

9
Long ē
Long ī

10
Long ē
Long ī

11
Long ē
Long ī

12
Long ē
Long ī

Y as Long i and Long e

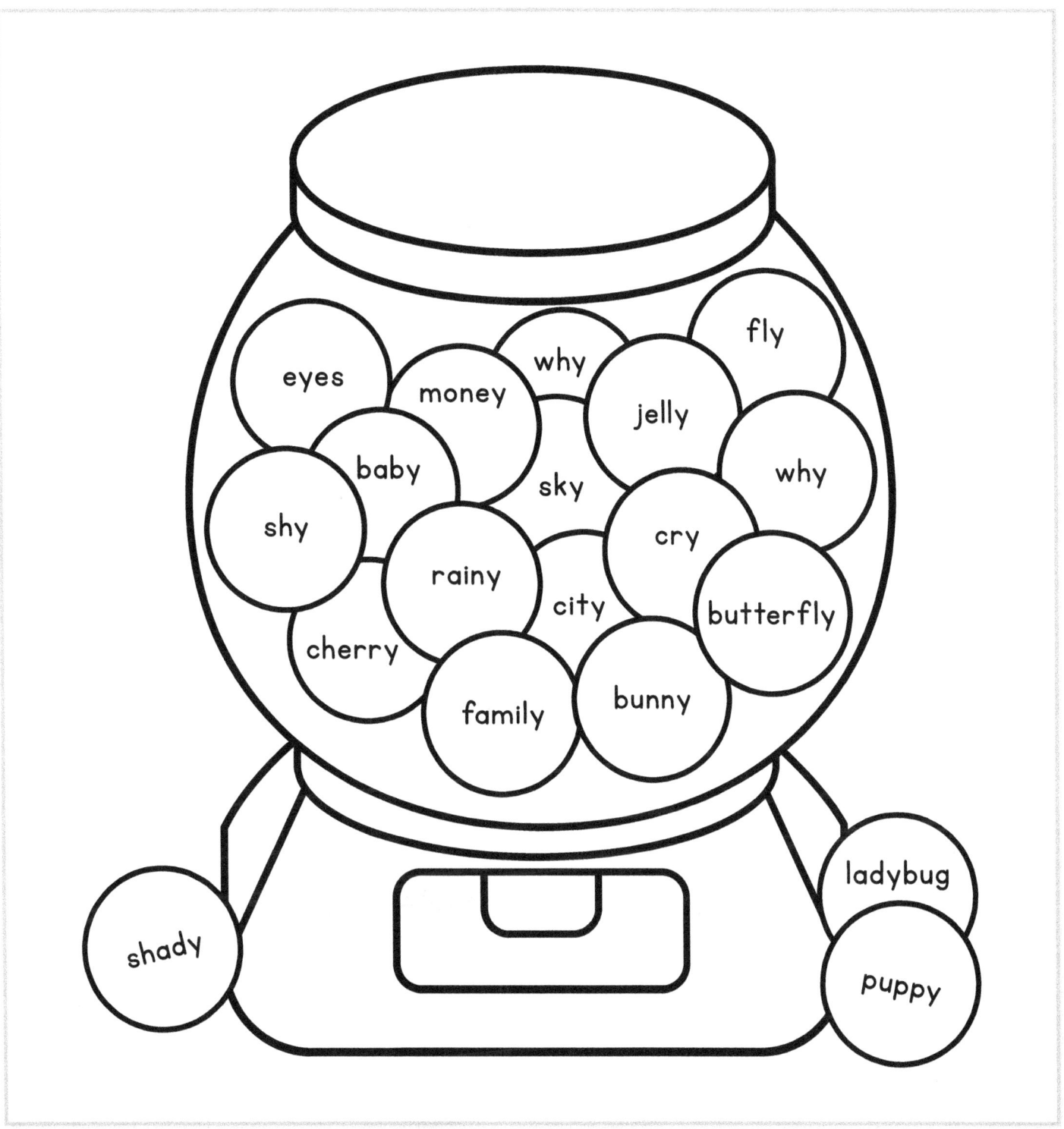

Colour the long ē words. orange
Colour the long ī words. green

Short and Long Vowels Review

Read the sentence.
Fill in the blank with the correct word for each sentence.

1 I _____ a sandwich for lunch today.　　**at / ate**

2 I _____ the weather is sunny.　　**hop / hope**

3 I picked up the _____ of toothpaste.　　**tub / tube**

4 My dad is wearing a red _____ on his head.　　**cap / cape**

5 I will get my hair _____ today.　　**cut / cute**

6 I am _____ at my friend.　　**mad / made**

7 I _____ do a handstand!　　**can / cane**

Short and Long Vowels Review

Read the sentence.
Fill in the blank with the correct word for each sentence.

1 My grandpa uses a _____ to walk.
can
cane

2 The kitten is small and very _____.
cut
cute

3 My parents _____ me clean my room.
mad
made

4 The little bunny can _____ very high!
hop
hope

5 A superhero wears a long _____.
cap
cape

6 The _____ is ready for my bubble bath.
tub
tube

7 There are many kids _____ school.
at
ate

Short and Long Vowels Review

Say the name of the object out loud. Draw a line from the object to the matching word. Colour the pictures.

1

cane   car

2

belt   leaf

3

pine   pig

4

bulb   fuel

5

mole   hog

6

cage   calf

7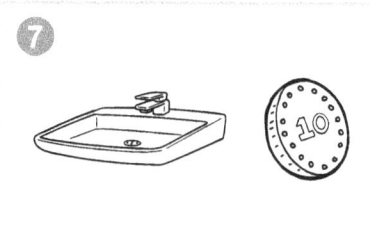

sink   dime

8

milk   dice

9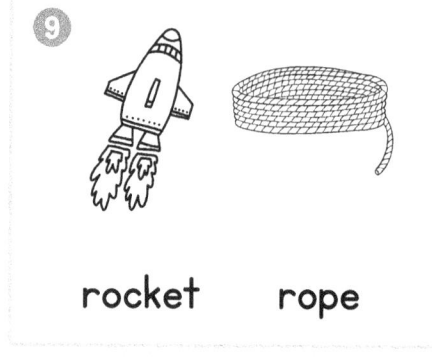

rocket   rope

10

drum   music

11

van   grapes

12

steps   steam

Short and Long Vowels Review

Say the name of the object out loud. Draw a line from the object to the matching word. Colour the pictures.

1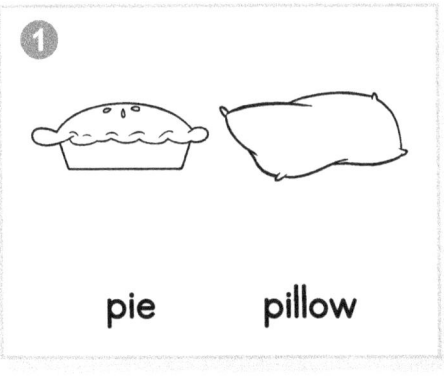
pie   pillow

2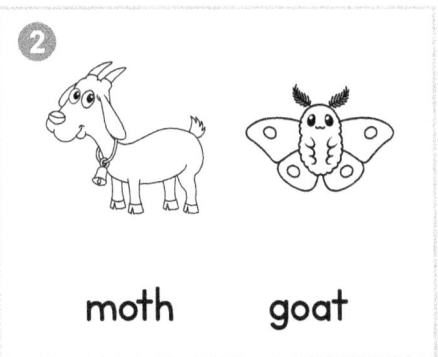
moth   goat

3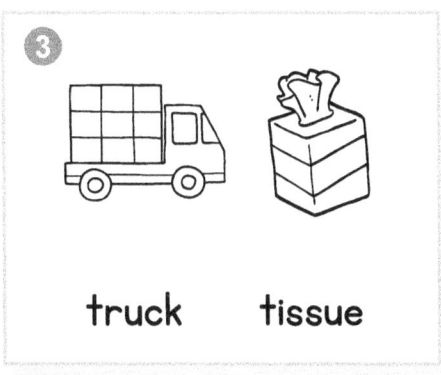
truck   tissue

4
cane   jam

5
letter   deer

6
igloo   flame

7
game   man

8
hen   seal

9
bike   swing

10
web   jeep

11
slippers   lion

12
box   comb

Short and Long Vowels Review

Say the name of the object out loud. Draw a line from the object to the matching word. Colour the pictures.

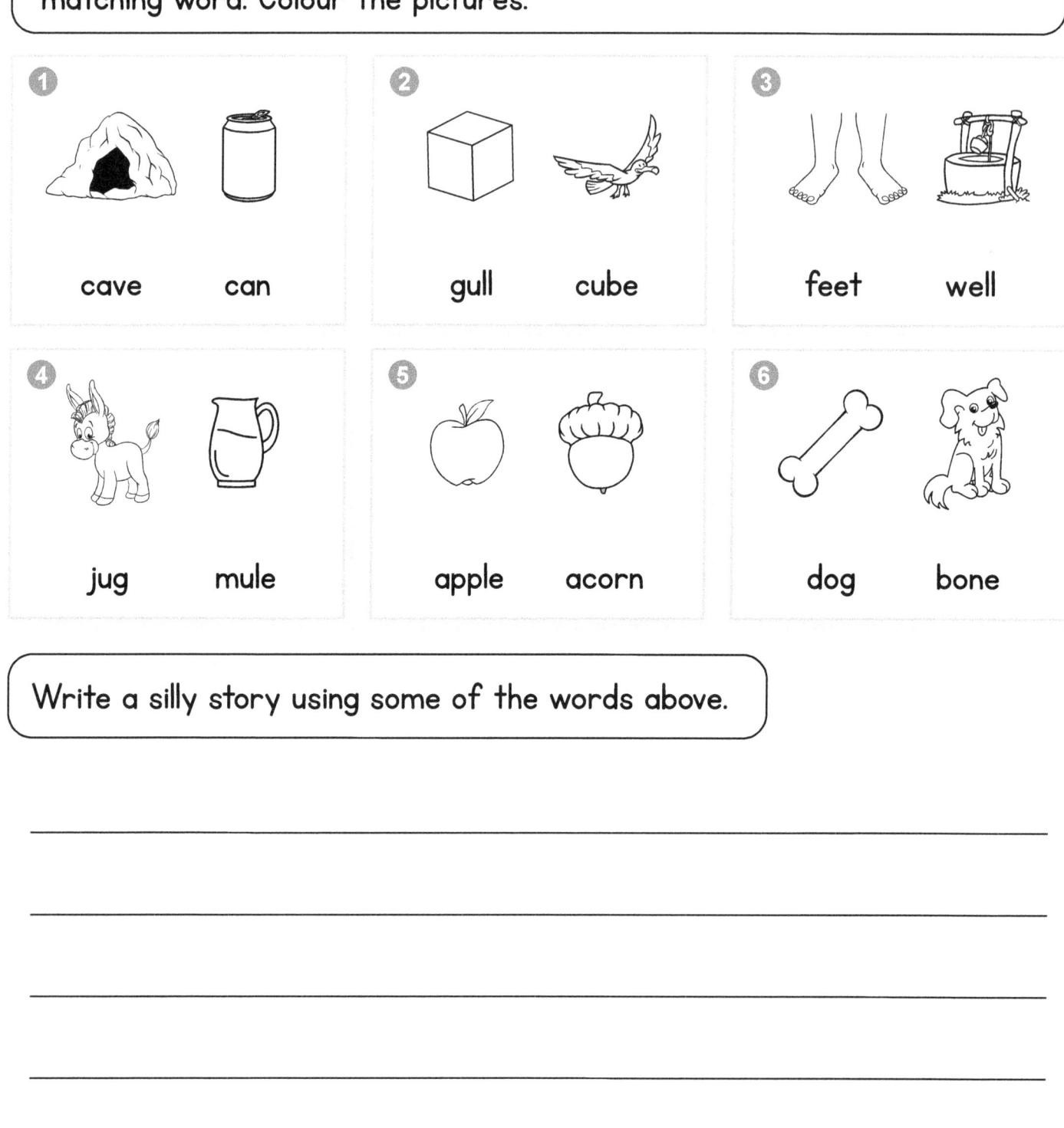

Write a silly story using some of the words above.

_____
_____
_____
_____
_____

☐ I used capitals and end marks.   ☐ My printing is neat.   ☐ My writing makes sense.

Consonant Blends

s blends

- **sk**eleton
- **sl**ice
- **sm**oke
- **sp**ider
- **sc**oop
- **sn**ail
- **st**airs
- **sw**ing

r blends

- **br**oom
- **gr**anny
- **cr**ayon
- **dr**um
- **fr**og
- **pr**inter
- **tr**ain

l blends

- **bl**ock
- **cl**own
- **gl**obe
- **fl**ower
- **pl**ant

Consonant Blends with s

Say the name of the object out loud.
Fill in the missing consonant blend or beginning sounds for the word.

1 sp   sl

____inner

2 sm   sk

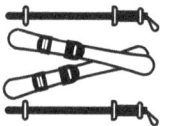

____is

3 sw   sn

____ail

4 sl   sp

____oon

5 sl   st

____ide

6 sn   sl

____ippers

7 sm   sc

____ell

8 sc   sk

____unk

9 sc   sp

____arf

10 sp   sk

____ull

11 sk   st

____ates

12 sc   st

____ar

Consonant Blends with s

Say the name of the object out loud.
Fill in the missing consonant blend or beginning sounds for the word.

1. sl   st
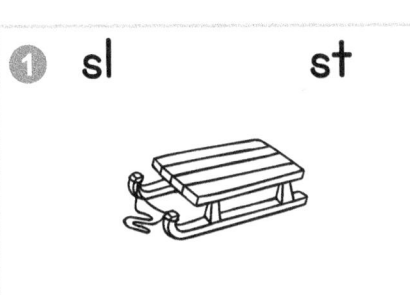
____ed

2. sm   sc
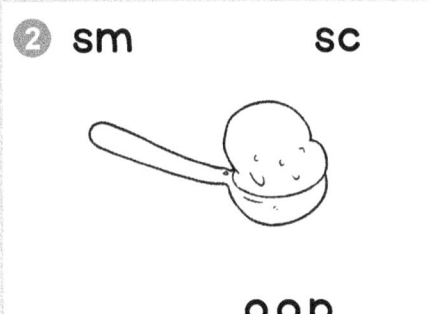
____oop

3. sp   sn
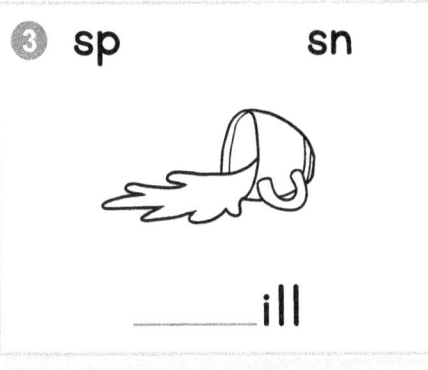
____ill

4. sn   sw

____an

5. sp   sk

____ider

6. st   sp
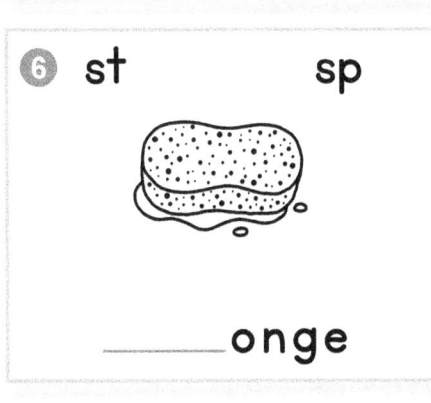
____onge

7. sw   sn
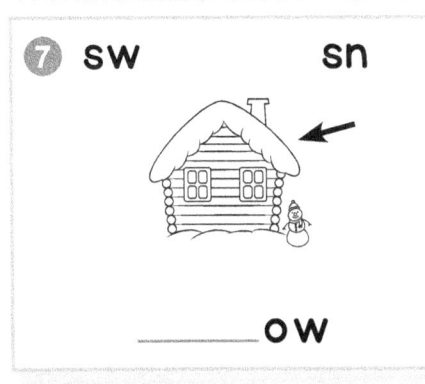
____ow

8. sw   sc
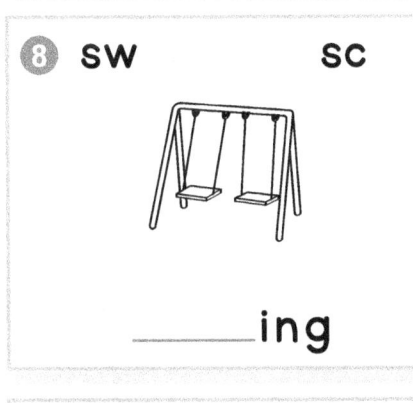
____ing

9. st   sk
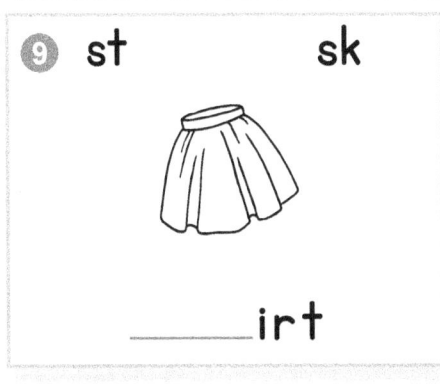
____irt

10. sm   sp
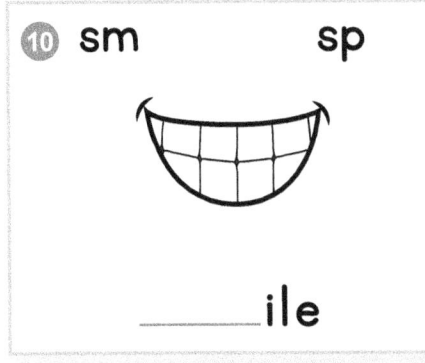
____ile

11. sk   sn

____eeze

12. sl   sp
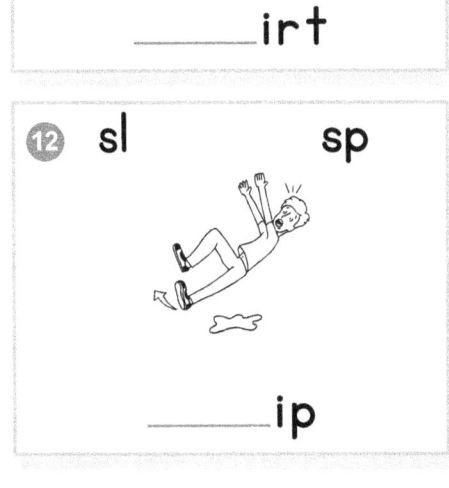
____ip

© Chalkboard Publishing Inc

Consonant Blends with s

Read the sentence and say the name of the object out loud. Fill in the blank with the missing consonant blend.

| sc | sl | sm | sn | st | sw |

1. My _____ippers are soft and fluffy.

2. The _____owman is smiling.

3. I like to _____ing in the park.

4. I use the _____oop for ice cream.

5. I put a _____amp on my letter.

6. _____oke comes from the campfire.

44

Consonant Blends with s

Read the sentence and say the name of the object out loud. Fill in the blank with the missing consonant blend.

| sc | sk | sl | sn | sp | st |

1 The ____ail moves very slowly.

2 My ____arf helps me keep warm.

3 I use a ____onge to clean the counter.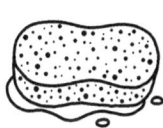

4 The ____ar has five points.

5 I will put on the ____ates.

6 I use a ____ed to go down the hill in winter.

Consonant Blends with s

Read the sentence and say the name of the object out loud. Fill in the blank with the missing consonant blend.

| sk | sl | sm | sn | sp | st |

① It's easy to accidently ___ill your drink.

② A ___oth moves very slowly.

③ When I am happy I ___ile.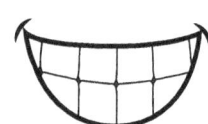

④ She ate an apple for her ___ack.

⑤ I wore a ___eleton costume for the party.

⑥ I like to sit on the ___eps and read.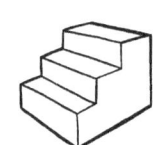

Consonant Blends with s

Read the sentence and say the name of the object out loud.
Fill in the blank with the missing consonant blend.

| sk | sl | sn | sp | st | sw |

1 The _____em holds the flower up.

2 The _____an is large and white.

3 The _____unk smells very bad!

4 Mom put orange _____ices on my plate.

5 I saw a _____ider in the attic.

6 Cover your face when you _____eeze.

Consonant Blends with r

Say the name of the object out loud.
Fill in the missing consonant blend or beginning sounds for the word.

1 br   fr

____idge

2 cr   gr

____anny

3 fr   dr

____ame

4 cr   dr

____ess

5 br   pr

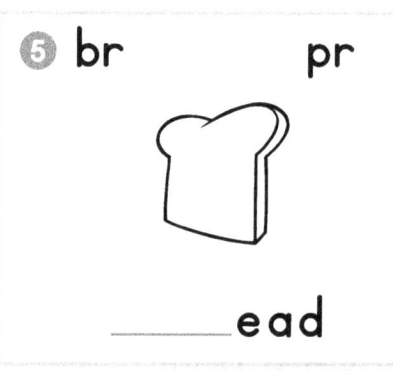

____ead

6 tr   gr

____apes

7 dr   cr

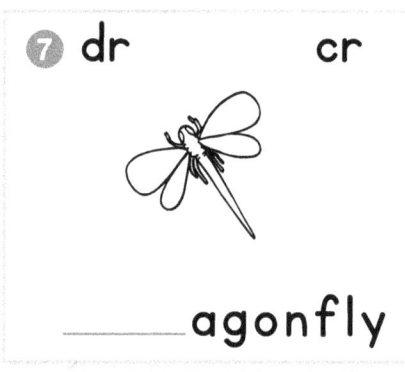

____agonfly

8 tr   pr

____ince

9 cr   dr

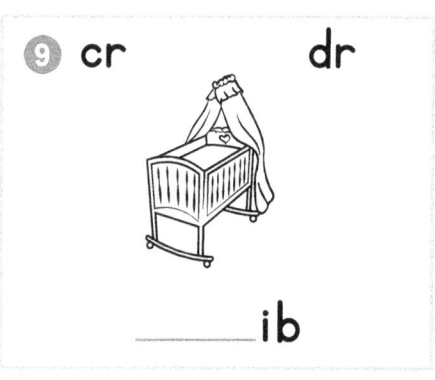

____ib

10 cr   fr

____own

11 tr   cr

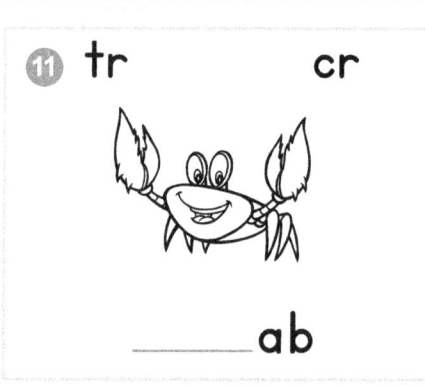

____ab

12 dr   pr

____um

Consonant Blends with r

Say the name of the object out loud.
Fill in the missing consonant blend or beginning sounds for the word.

① br   gr

___oom

② dr   fr

___og

③ cr   pr
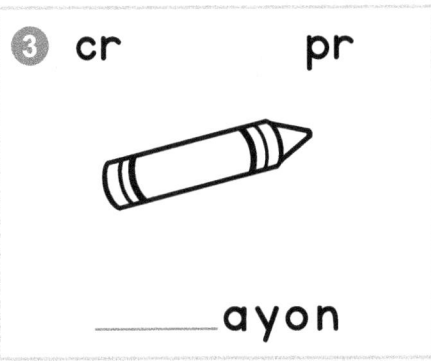
___ayon

④ br   cr

___ane

⑤ dr   gr

___agon

⑥ fr   tr
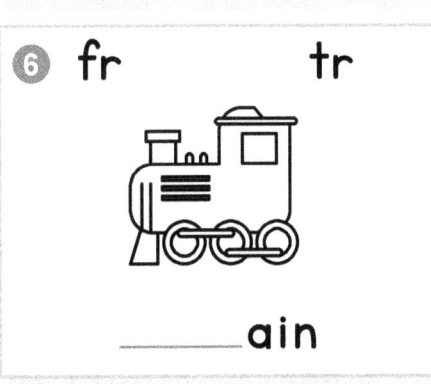
___ain

⑦ pr   cr
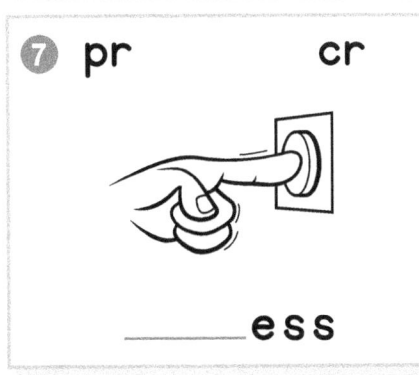
___ess

⑧ br   fr

___iends

⑨ cr   dr

___ink

⑩ pr   tr
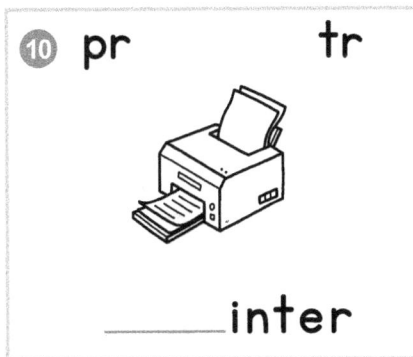
___inter

⑪ cr   fr
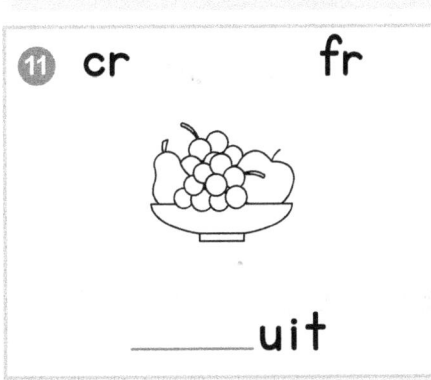
___uit

⑫ tr   br
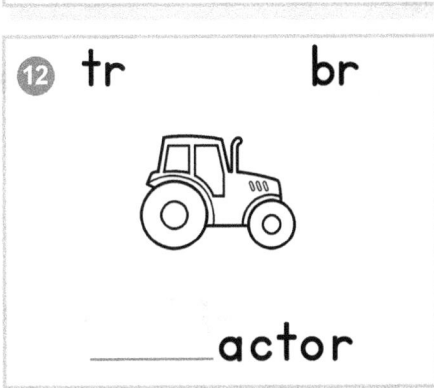
___actor

Consonant Blends with r

Read the sentence and say the name of the object out loud.
Fill in the blank with the missing consonant blend.

| br | cr | dr | fr | gr | pr |

1. The _____ead is soft and fresh.

2. The _____ane lifts heavy things.

3. I like to spend time with my _____iend.

4. The little _____agon is friendly.

5. I want to _____ess the button.

6. _____apes are sweet and tasty.

50 © Chalkboard Publishing Inc

Consonant Blends with r

Read the sentence and say the name of the object out loud. Fill in the blank with the missing consonant blend.

| br | cr | dr | fr | gr | tr |

1

The ____ayon is red.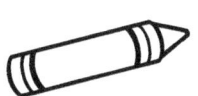

2

I want to ride on a ____ain!

3

I use the ____oom to sweep the floor.

4

I would like a ____ink.

5

I want to put a picture in the ____ame.

6

I love to visit my ____anny!

Consonant Blends with r

Read the sentence and say the name of the object out loud. Fill in the blank with the missing consonant blend.

| br | cr | dr | gr | pr | tr |

1. A big green _____actor is used on the farm.

2. The stone _____idge is very long!

3. My Uncle Tim grows _____apes.

4. The red _____agonfly moves quickly.

5. The _____ince is a kind boy.

6. Little blue _____ab ran over the sand.

Consonant Blends with r

Read the sentence and say the name of the object out loud. Fill in the blank with the missing consonant blend.

| cr | dr | fr | gr | pr | tr |

1

My story came out of the _____ inter.

2

The baby sleeps in the _____ ib.

3

The little _____ og swims in the pond.

4

The _____ ess is bright yellow.

5

My mom has a big _____ in on her face.

6

My uncle drives a _____ uck.

© Chalkboard Publishing Inc

Consonant Blends with l

Say the name of the object out loud.
Fill in the missing consonant blend or beginning sounds for the word.

1 bl cl

____ackboard

2 pl fl
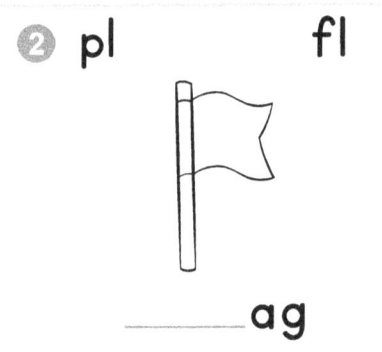
____ag

3 bl cl

____own

4 pl bl

____ane

5 fl gl
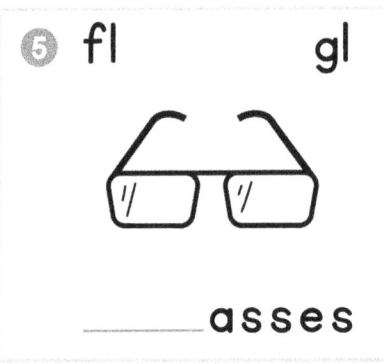
____asses

6 cl pl
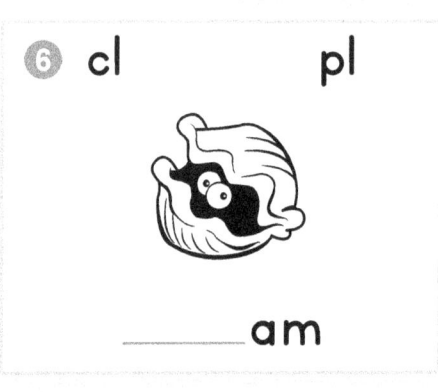
____am

7 gl fl
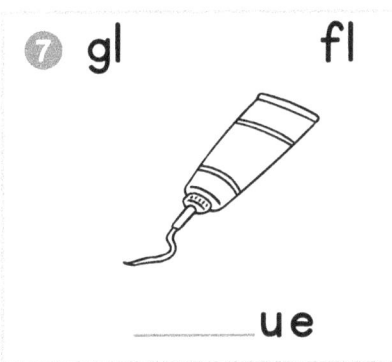
____ue

8 bl fl

____ender

9 cl fl

____ower

10 bl pl
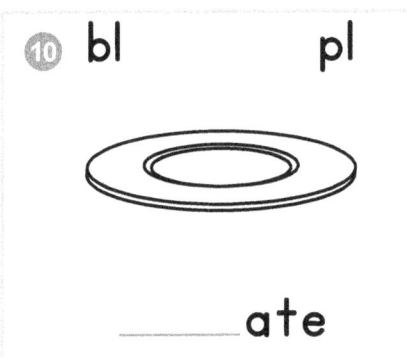
____ate

11 cl gl

____over

12 fl pl

____ame

Consonant Blends with l

Say the name of the object out loud.
Fill in the missing consonant blend or beginning sounds for the word.

1. bl   pl

____ow

2. pl   cl
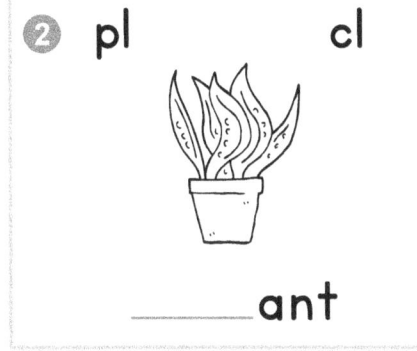
____ant

3. fl   gl
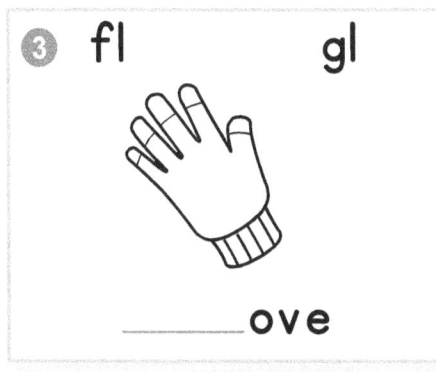
____ove

4. fl   pl
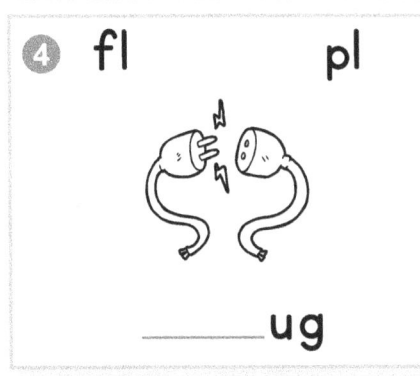
____ug

5. gl   bl

____obe

6. bl   cl
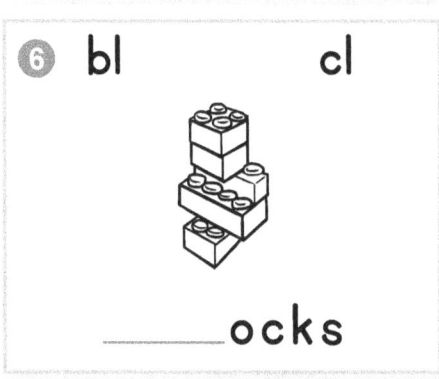
____ocks

7. fl   gl
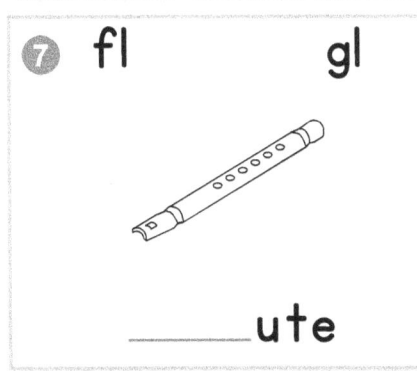
____ute

8. bl   pl
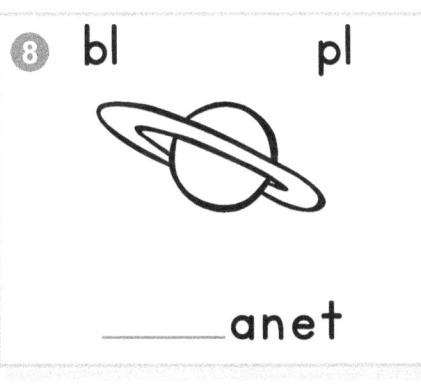
____anet

9. gl   pl
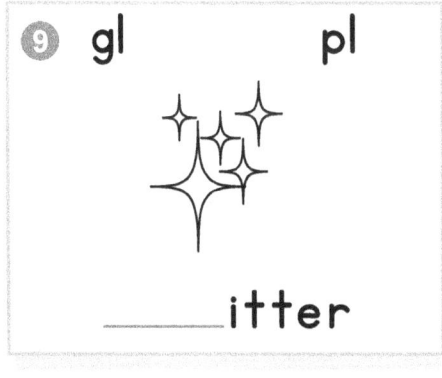
____itter

10. cl   fl

____oud

11. bl   cl
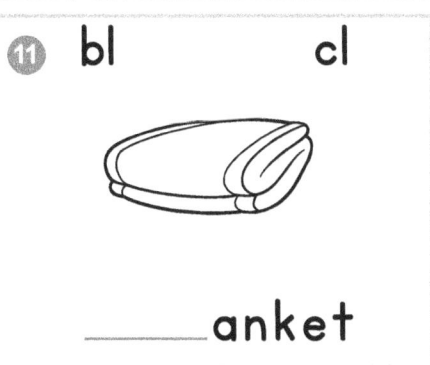
____anket

12. pl   fl
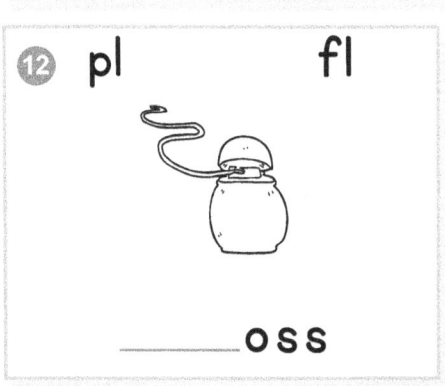
____oss

© Chalkboard Publishing Inc

Consonant Blends with l

Read the sentence and say the name of the object out loud. Fill in the blank with the missing consonant blend.

1. My brother can play the _____ute.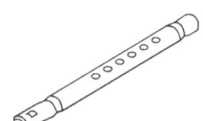

2. The _____anket keeps me warm!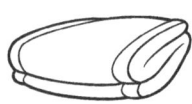

3. I added lots of _____itter on the card.

4. A _____over with four leaves is lucky.

5. The _____ue is very sticky.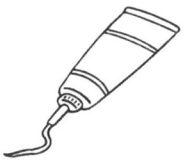

6. The _____anet has a big ring around it.

Consonant Blends with l

Read the sentence and say the name of the object out loud. Fill in the blank with the missing consonant blend.

| bl | cl | fl | gl | pl |

1

I ate a _____um for a snack.

2

I like to play with building _____ocks!

3

The _____obe shows the whole world!

4

I _____oss my teeth every day.

5

My mom made us drinks with the _____ender.

6

I saw a _____oud shaped like a cat.

Consonant Blends with l

Read the sentence and say the name of the object out loud. Fill in the blank with the missing consonant blend.

bl   cl   fl   gl   pl

1. I wrote my name on the _____ackboard.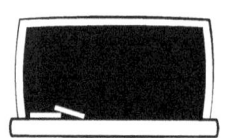

2. The _____am has a hard shell.

3. I always wash my _____ate.

4. The _____ower smells very sweet.

5. My friend wears _____asses to help him see.

6. Always be careful around an open _____ame.

Consonant Blends with l

Read the sentence and say the name of the object out loud.
Fill in the blank with the missing consonant blend.

| bl | cl | fl | gl | pl |

1

The _____ane was high in the sky.

2

We put a _____ag on our box fort.

3

The _____own was very funny!

4

A strong wind may _____ow things over!

5

I water the _____ant every week.

6

We found Canada on the _____obe.

Consonant Blends Review

Say the name of the object out loud.
Fill in the missing consonant blend or beginning sounds for the word.

1. br   fr

____idge

2. gl   bl
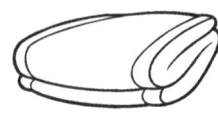
____anket

3. pl   sl

____ug

4. sl   sw

____ing

5. br   sl

____ead

6. sp   sm

____ell

7. sn   fr

____eeze

8. fl   sl
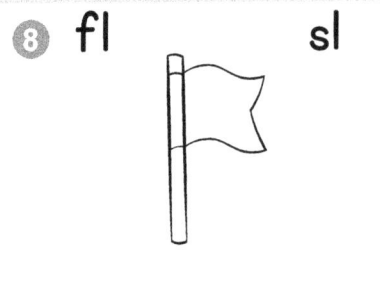
____ag

9. sp   st

____ill

10. cr   fr

____own

11. dr   cr

____ab

12. br   bl

____ocks

Consonant Blends Review

Say the name of the object out loud.
Fill in the missing consonant blend or beginning sounds for the word.

1 sp sk

____unk

2 cl bl

____ock

3 pr pl
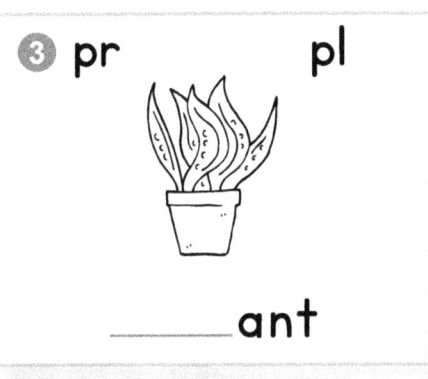
____ant

4 sc st
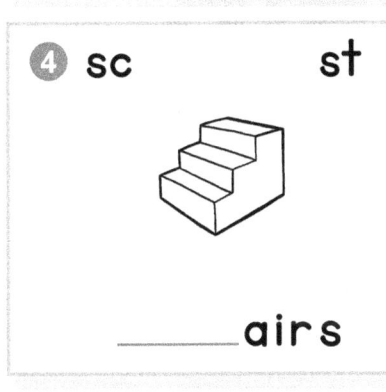
____airs

5 gl gr
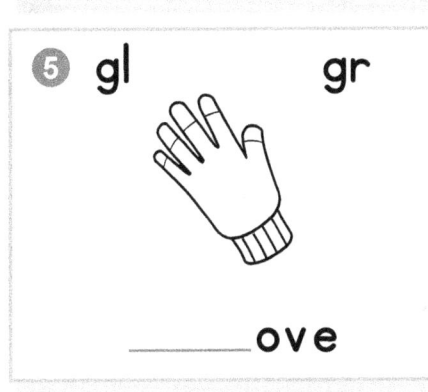
____ove

6 bl fr

____iend

7 dr gr

____anny

8 sk pl
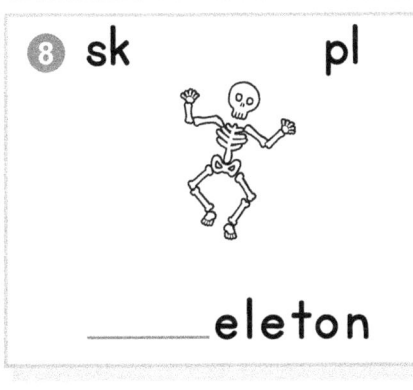
____eleton

9 pr br

____oom

10 tr pl

____ain

11 sp st
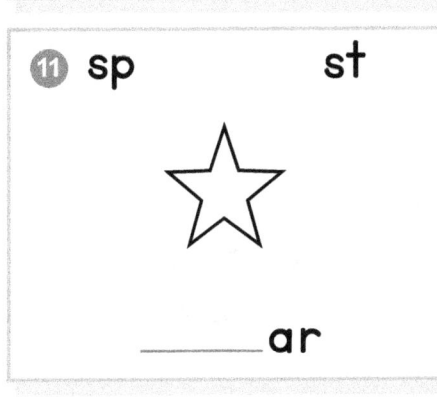
____ar

12 fl sl

____y

Hard c and Soft c Sounds

Hard *c* sound:
The letter *c* makes a *k* sound when followed by the letters *a*, *o*, or *u*.

cat

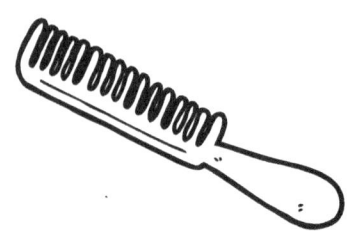
comb

Soft *c* sound:
The letter *c* makes an *s* sound when followed by the letters *i*, *e*, or *y*.

city

cent

Circle all the words with a hard *c* sound.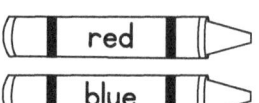
Circle all the words with a soft *c* sound.

Hard c and Soft c Sounds

Say the name of the object out loud.
Use the colour key to colour the pictures.

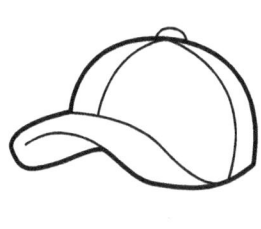
cap

pencil

coat

mice

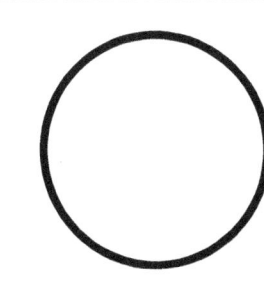
circle

celery

cake

cup

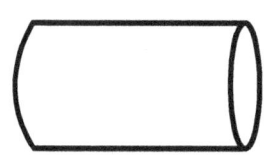
cylinder

Circle all the words with a hard *c* sound. 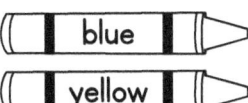 blue
Circle all the words with a soft *c* sound. yellow

Hard c and Soft c Sounds

1 Read each word out loud.
Sort the hard *c* and soft *c* words by writing them in the correct box.

| camel | circus | cookie | cupcake | icy |
| lettuce | music | octagon | space | voice |

hard c words

soft c words

2 Unscramble the word.

a) yci _____

b) mleac _____

c) cvioe _____

d) pesac _____

e) cucris _____

f) icsum _____

Hard c and Soft c Sounds

3 Fill in the blank using the best word from the list.

| can | candle | card | castle | cereal |
| cider | cold | pencil | recess | rice |

a. Emma ate a bowl of _____ for breakfast.

b. Alex likes to eat _____ with mushrooms.

c. The king and queen live in the _____.

d. The birthday _____ played a song for me.

e. I can't wait to go out for _____ and play.

f. Wax drips down the side of the _____.

g. It is very _____ outside in the winter.

h. Sharpen your _____ before you print.

i. Would you like some apple _____ to drink?

j. Mom opened a _____ of soup for lunch.

Hard g and Soft g Sounds

Hard *g* sound:
The hard *g* sound has the sound of *g* as in the word *goat*.

gull

garden

Soft *g* sound:
The soft *g* sound has the sound of *j* as in the word *cage*.

gem

gingerbread

Circle all the words with a hard *g* sound.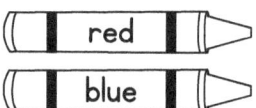
Circle all the words with a soft *g* sound.

Hard g and Soft g Sounds

Say the name of the object out loud.
Use the colour key to colour the pictures.

goat

goose

gingerbread

gum

giraffe

gull

gem

genius

gate

Circle all the words with a hard *g* sound. 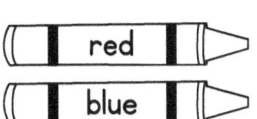 red
Circle all the words with a soft *g* sound. blue

Hard and Soft g Sounds

1 Read each word out loud.
Sort the hard **g** and soft **g** words by writing them in the correct box.

| bridge | cage | frog | flag | gentle |
| germ | gift | girl | goldfish | magic |

hard g words

soft g words

2 Unscramble the word.

a) **lfga** _____   b) **gbdier** _____

c) **aigcm** _____   d) **rlgi** _____

e) **remg** _____   f) **eglnte** _____

Hard and Soft g Sounds

3) Fill in the blank using the best word from the list.

| age | change | garden | giant | gift |
| giraffe | goal | gorilla | guitar | gym |

a) What is the _____ of this dinosaur bone?

b) The leaves _____ colours in the fall.

c) Sara bought a birthday _____ for her friend.

d) The _____ slide was fun to go down.

e) A _____ can be as tall as a tree.

f) We played dodgeball in _____ class.

g) My sister played a song on her _____ .

h) My _____ is to read five pages every day.

i) We will plant tulips in our flower _____ this year.

j) A _____ ran away with the bananas.

Final Consonant Blends: st and sk

1 Read each word out loud.
Sort the words by writing them in the correct box.

desk	dust	fast	flask	past
rest	risk	task	twist	whisk

___ *st* words

___ *sk* words

2 Unscramble the word.

a) **eksd** _____

b) **itwts** _____

c) **usdt** _____

d) **rets** _____

e) **srki** _____

f) **asft** _____

Final Consonant Blends: st and sk

3 Fill in the blank using the best word from the list.

| ask | best | breakfast | frost | husk |
| list | lost | mask | past | whisk |

a. I like to eat cereal for _____.

b. You must _____ the corn before cooking it.

c. My mom _____ her keys.

d. Dad beat the eggs with a _____.

e. Look at the _____ on the window.

f. I will _____ my mom if I can go to the party.

g. Ben put on a silly monkey _____.

h. It is _____ my bedtime.

i. Please make a _____ of things you need.

j. My _____ friend is Carlos.

Final Consonant Blends: nd, nk, and nt

1 Read each word out loud.
Sort the words by writing them in the correct box.

blend	chant	honk	plant	rink
round	sand	shrink	tent	want

___ **nd** words	___ **nk** words	___ **nt** words

2 Write a sentence using a word from each list.

Final Consonant Blends: nd, nk, and nt

3 Fill in the blank using the best word from the list.

| bank | diamond | friend | junk | pink |
| pond | print | round | sand | skunk |

a. My best _____ is Mary.

b. The ducks swam in the _____ .

c. _____ your name at the top of the page.

d. We played in the _____ at the beach.

e. The crown has one _____ and three pearls.

f. I want a _____ birthday cake.

g. My sister's favourite colour is _____ .

h. The fluffy _____ raced into the bushes.

i. What time will the _____ open?

j. Billy never eats _____ food.

Words with sh and ch

1. Say each word out loud.
   Listen for the **sh** sound or the **ch** sound.

| catch | chain | couch | dish | ketchup |
| mushroom | ostrich | shell | shout | shrimp |

sh words

ch words

2. Write a sentence using a word from each list.

Words with sh and ch

3 Fill in the blank using the best word from the list.

| beach | cheese | chess | fish | lunch |
| sheep | ship | sunshine | teacher | trash |

a We put out the _____ on Sunday nights.

b Bob feeds his pet _____ every morning.

c I am learning how to play _____ .

d Try counting _____ to go to sleep.

e I am going to eat a sandwich for _____ .

f I like _____ on my hamburger.

g My grandmother will travel here by _____ .

h My _____ helps me with math.

i I like the warm _____ on my skin.

j We are going to the _____ this weekend.

Words with th and wh

1. Say each word out loud.
   Listen for the *th* sound or the *wh* sound.

| birthday | month | wheat | think | thousand |
| tooth | what | wheel | where | why |

***th* words**	***wh* words**

2. Write a sentence using a word from each list.

_____

_____

_____

Words with th and wh

3 Fill in the blank using the best word from the list.

| Earth | feather | thirsty | thunder | what |
| wheat | wheel | where | why | with |

a. We live on planet _____.

b. Can you hear the _____?

c. The balloon is light as a _____.

d. I am going to the movies _____ my brother.

e. _____ do I have to get up so early?

f. A unicycle has one _____.

g. My uncle grows _____ on his farm.

h. _____ did I put my backpack?

i. _____ time do we have to leave for the play?

j. I like to drink water when I am _____.

Silent Letters

1 Say the word out loud. Pay attention to which letters you can't hear. Print the letter or letters you can't hear beside the word.

knee _____   walk _____   two _____

honest _____   comb _____   ghost _____

race _____   knit _____   dime _____

climb _____   answer _____   calf _____

2 Sort the words above into the correct box.

Words with a silent **b**	Words with a silent **e**	Words with a silent **k**

Words with a silent **h**	Words with a silent **l**	Words with a silent **w**

Silent Letters

3 Say each word out loud. Pay attention to which letters you can't hear. Print the word that has a silent letter.

a) knob   kite   _____

b) dance   door   _____

c) two   tulip   _____

d) crumb   cook   _____

e) talk   camp   _____

4 Say the name of the object out loud. Fill in the missing silent consonant.

a)
____night

b)
com____

c)
g____ost

d) ca____f

Vowel Pairs: er, ir, ur

1 Say each word out loud.
Listen to the sounds the letters *er*, *ir*, and *ur* make.
Sort the *er*, *ir*, and *ur* words by writing them in the correct box.

bird	burn	curl	first	flower
girl	hammer	letter	mother	nurse
purse	shirt	skirt	tiger	turn

er words	*ir* words	*ur* words

2 Write the word from the list that rhymes with the bold word.

a) **skirt** _____   b) **turn** _____

c) **girl** _____   d) **nurse** _____

Vowel Pairs: er, ir, ur

3. Say the name of the object out loud.
Write the letters **er**, **ir**, or **ur** to complete the word.

a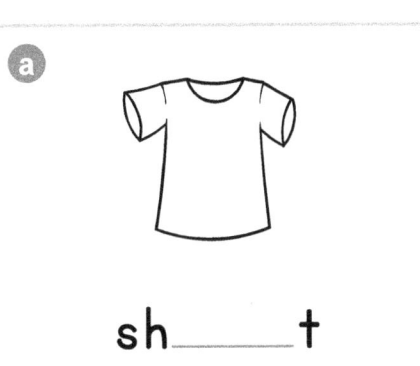
sh____t

b
p____se

c
hamm____

d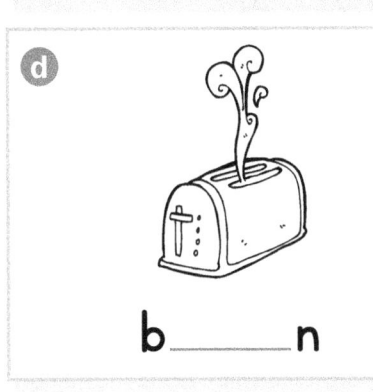
b____n

e
b____d

f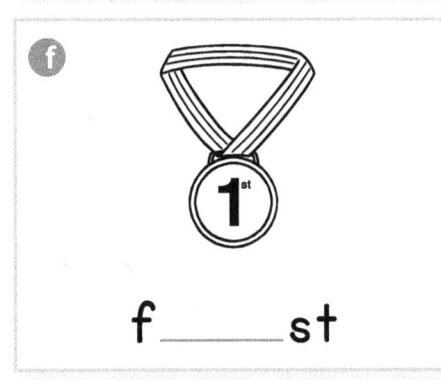
f____st

g
flow____

h
t____tle

i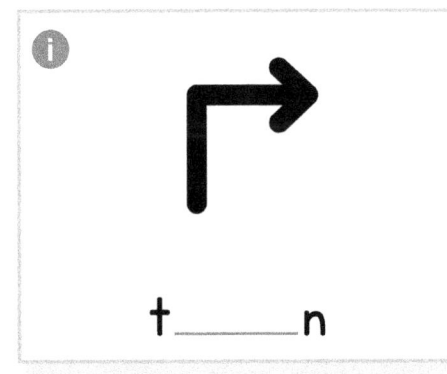
t____n

j
lett____

k
sk____t

l
tig____

Vowel Pairs: ar and or

1 Say each word out loud.
Listen to the sounds the letters **ar** and **or** make.
Sort the **ar** and **or** words by writing them in the correct box.

| art | carpet | cord | farm | fork |
| garden | horse | mark | sport | sword |

***ar* words**	***or* words**

2 Circle the words that rhyme with the bold word.

a) **art**   start   heat   smart

b) **chord**   sword   afford   reset

Vowel Pairs: ar and or

3. Say the name of the object out loud.
   Write the letters **ar** or **or** to complete the word.

a
b____n

b
c____d

c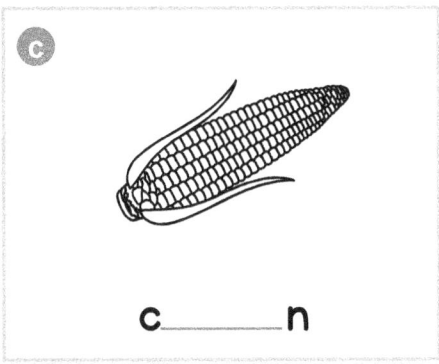
c____n

d
f____k

e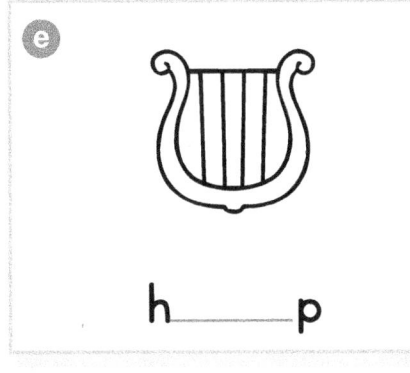
h____p

f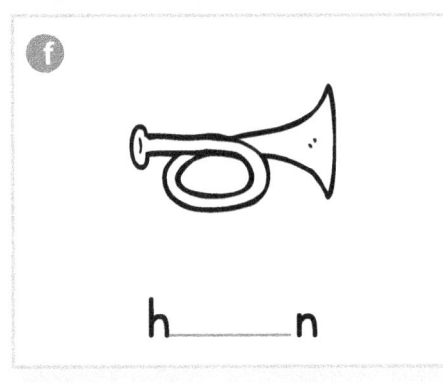
h____n

g
h____se

h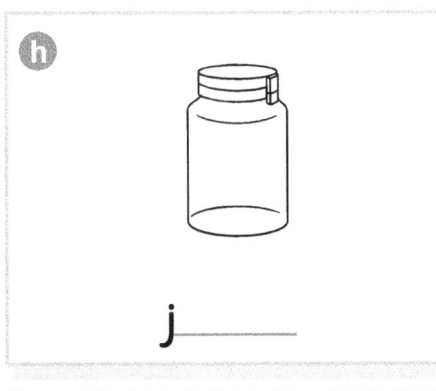
j____

i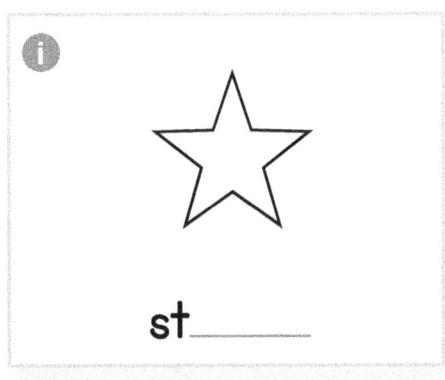
st____

j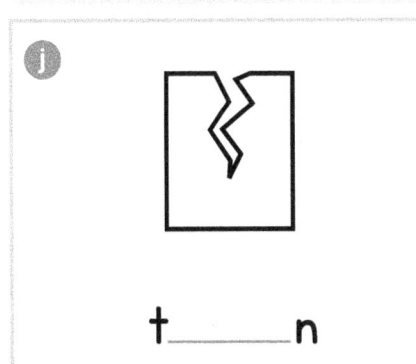
t____n

k
sh____k

l
st____m

Vowel Pairs: ai and ay

1 Read each word out loud.
Listen to the sounds the letters *ai* and *ay* make.
Notice how they make the same sound.
Sort the *ai* and *ay* words by writing them in the correct box.

| brain | clay | daisy | day | nail |
| play | rain | snail | stay | tray |

ai words	*ay* words

2 Circle the words that rhyme with the bold word.

a) **play**   tray   stay   plate

b) **nail**   mail   boil   sail

Vowel Pairs: ai and ay

3. Fill in the blank using the best word from the list.

| drain | holiday | mail | May | paid |
| paint | play | rainbow | snail | today |

a. Evan _____ three dollars for new hockey cards.

b. Thanksgiving is my favourite _____.

c. The water goes down the _____.

d. My mom will _____ my letter to my Grandma.

e. I love to _____ in art class.

f. A _____ moves very slowly.

g. There are many colours in a _____.

h. _____ we are going to the library.

i. Can I go out to _____

j. My birthday is in the month of _____.

Vowel Pairs: oi and oy

1 Read each word out loud.
Listen to the sounds the letters *oi* and *oy* make.
Notice how they make the same sound.
Sort the *oi* and *oy* words by writing them in the correct box.

| boil | joy | join | loyal | oyster |
| point | royal | soil | toy | voice |

oi words	*oy* words

2 Circle the words that rhyme with the bold word.

a) **toy**   boy   joy   royal

b) **soil**   point   boil   foil

Vowel Pairs: oi and oy

3 Fill in the blank using the best word from the list.

| boy | coin | enjoy | join | loyal |
| noise | oil | oyster | soil | toy |

a. I really _____ playing with my friends.

b. Flip a _____ to see who will go first.

c. The _____ next door is moving away.

d. The flowers grow well in this _____ .

e. We need to change the _____ in our car.

f. Please _____ us for supper tonight.

g. A good friend is a person who is _____ to you.

h. My _____ boat floats in water.

i. What is that _____ I hear outside?

j. There is a pearl inside the _____ .

Vowel Pairs: au and aw

1 Read each word out loud.
Listen to the sounds the letters **au** and **aw** make.
Notice how they make the same sound.
Sort the **au** and **aw** words by writing them in the correct box.

| autumn | because | claw | draw | faucet |
| launch | pause | raw | straw | yawn |

au words	*aw* words

2 Write a sentence using a word from each list.

Vowel Pairs: au and aw

3 Fill in the blank using the best word from the list.

August	author	crawl	draw	faucet
lawn	Paul	paw	raw	sauce

a. An _____ writes books for a living.

b. The grass on my _____ is green.

c. My friend's name is _____.

d. I like to put extra _____ on my pasta.

e. I like to _____ pictures in my sketchbook.

f. My baby brother can _____.

g. It is not safe to eat _____ meats.

h. _____ is my favourite month.

i. Water pours out of the _____.

j. My cat put her _____ on my head.

Vowel Pairs: ou and ow

1 Read each word out loud.
Listen to the sounds the letters **ou** and **ow** make.
Notice how they make the same sound.
Sort the **ou** and **ow** words by writing them in the correct box.

| couch | down | flower | gown | loud |
| mouse | mouth | owl | power | shout |

ou words

ow words

_____

2 Circle the words that rhyme with the bold word.

a) **flower**   power   cloud   tower

b) **mouse**   blouse   house   mother

Vowel Pairs: ou and ow

3 Fill in the blank using the best word from the list.

| about | brown | cloud | clown | down |
| found | hour | loud | now | town |

a Piper is reading a book _____ fish.

b What was that _____ sound? It scared me!

c I need to be home in an _____ .

d Lucy _____ her missing shoe under her bed.

e We need to leave _____ , or we will be late.

f My pet dog's fur is light _____ .

g Andrew lives just _____ the street from me.

h There is not a _____ in the blue sky.

i My cousins live in a very small _____ .

j There was a funny _____ at the party.

Vowel Pairs: ee and ea

1. Read each word out loud.
   Listen to the sounds the letters **ee** and **ea** make.
   Notice how they make the same middle sound as in feet and meat.
   Sort the **ee** and **ea** words by writing them in the correct box.

feet	tree	seek	seed	leaf
mean	read	team	steal	sheep

ee words	**ea** words

2. Circle the words that rhyme with the bold word.

   a. **sheep**   jeep   sheet   deep

   b. **team**   tear   cream   dream

Vowel Pairs: ee and ea

3 Fill in the blank using the best word from the list.

beach	clean	east	feed	jeans
sleep	teeth	week	meal	leaf

a) Go brush your _____.

b) Dinner is my favourite _____ of the day.

c) My blue _____ have a rip in the knee.

d) Jill lives in the _____ end of the city.

e) Don't forget to _____ the fish.

f) We built a sand castle on the _____.

g) There are seven days in a _____.

h) My chore is to put away the _____ laundry.

i) I saw a _____ fall off the tree.

j) Breanna counts _____ to help her go to sleep.

Vowel Pairs: oa and ow

1 Read each word out loud.
Listen to the sounds the letters *oa* and *ow* make.
Notice how they make the same middle sound as in boat and snow.
Sort the *oa* and *ow* words by writing them in the correct box.

| boat | bow | blow | coat | follow |
| road | soap | snow | glow | toast |

oa words	*ow* words

2 Circle the words that rhyme with the bold word.

a) **coat**   oat   cow   goat

b) **bow**   show   boot   blow

Vowel Pairs: oa and ow

3. Fill in the blank using the best word from the list.

bowl	float	goat	loaf	soap
pillow	show	toast	yellow	throw

a. I like butter and jam on _____.

b. It is fun to _____ in the pool.

c. What are you bringing for _____ and tell?

d. My favourite colour is _____.

e. The billy _____ eats grass.

f. Grandma just baked a fresh _____ of bread.

g. I had a _____ of soup with my lunch.

h. I want to rest my head on the _____.

i. Use _____ to wash your hands.

j. _____ Scott the ball.

Vowel Pairs: Long oo and Short oo

1. Read each word out loud.
   Sort the short **oo** and long **oo** words by writing them in the correct box.

| book | foot | took | soon | hook |
| boot | tooth | cool | food | wool |

Long **oo**	Short **oo**

2. Circle the words that rhyme with the bold word.

a. **loose**   goose   blouse   moose

b. **took**   take   shook   hook

Vowel Pairs: Long oo and Short oo

3 Fill in the blank using the best word from the list.

| choose | cook | look | loose | took |
| good | roof | spoon | moon | wool |

a) I have a _____ tooth.

b) Sam needs a _____ to eat his soup.

c) The _____ of the house is leaking.

d) I hope you had a _____ day.

e) The _____ is out tonight.

f) My dad is a great _____ .

g) _____ an outfit to wear for tomorrow.

h) _____ over your answers carefully.

i) My _____ sweater is very warm and cozy.

j) I _____ my little sister to the park.

Vowel Pairs: ew and ui

① Say each word out loud.
Listen to the sounds the letters *ew* and *ui* make.
Sort the *ew* and *ui* words by writing them in the correct box.

| chew | cruise | few | fruit |
| grew | juice | new | suit |

ew words

ui words

② Print a word that rhymes with each bold word.

a. **cruise** _____

b. **fruit** _____

c. **blew** _____

Vowel Pairs: ew and ui

3 Fill in the blank using the best word from the list.

| chew | cruise | flew | fruit | recruit |
| grew | juice | new | suit | fluids |

a. My aunt is going on a boat _____.

b. Grapes and apples are tasty in _____ salad.

c. My plant _____ 3 cm in one month.

d. I love to drink fresh orange _____.

e. The airplane _____ over our heads.

f. My parents bought me a _____ game!

g. Always be sure to _____ your food.

h. My dad wears a fancy _____.

i. The hockey coach wants to _____ new players.

j. When you have a cold, drink lots of _____.

Vowel Pairs Review

Say the name of the object out loud.
Fill in the missing vowel pair for the word.

1 oa   ow

s____p

2 ar   or
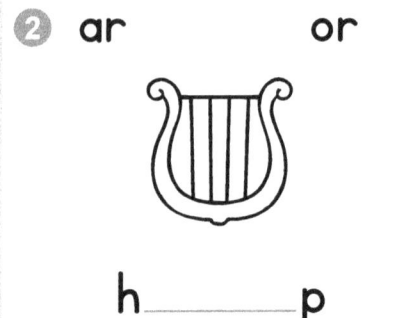
h____p

3 oi   oy
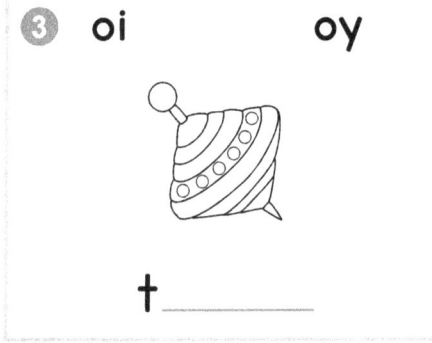
t____

4 au   aw
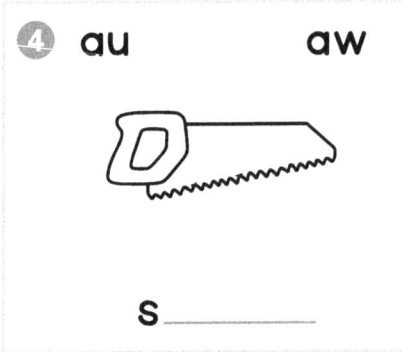
s____

5 ee   ea
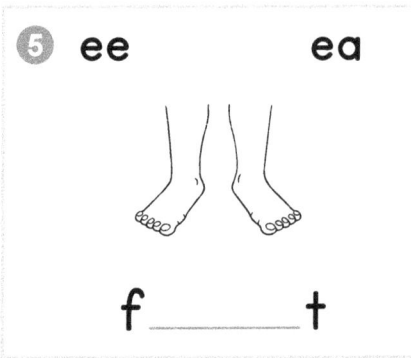
f____t

6 oa   ow
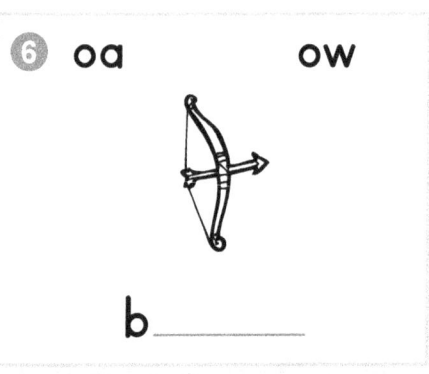
b____

7 er   ir
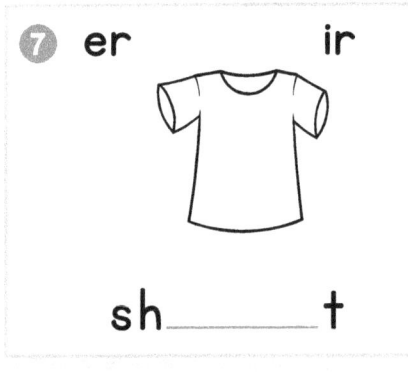
sh____t

8 oi   oy
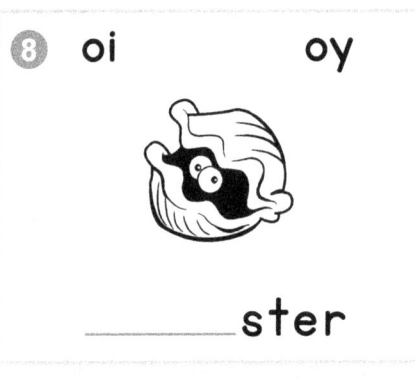
____ster

9 ou   ow
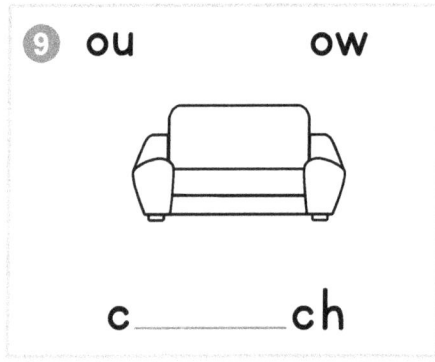
c____ch

10 ir   ur

b____d

11 ew   ui
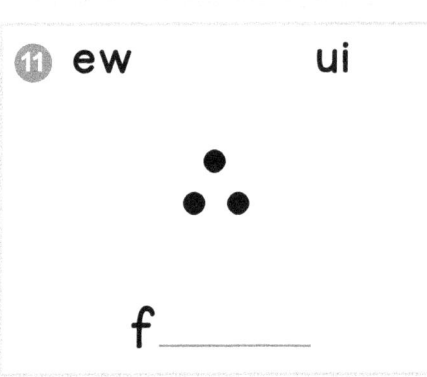
f____

12 er   ur

lett____

Vowel Pairs Review

Say the name of the object out loud.
Fill in the missing vowel pair for the word.

1. oa   ow
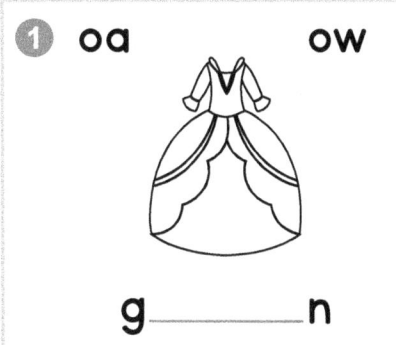
g_____n

2. ui   eu
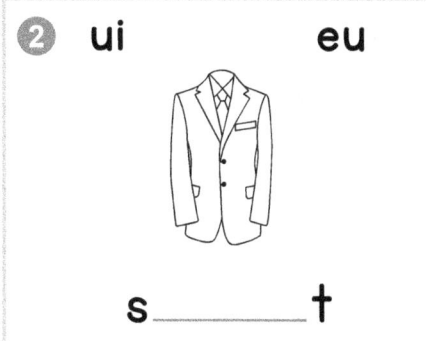
s_____t

3. ee   ea
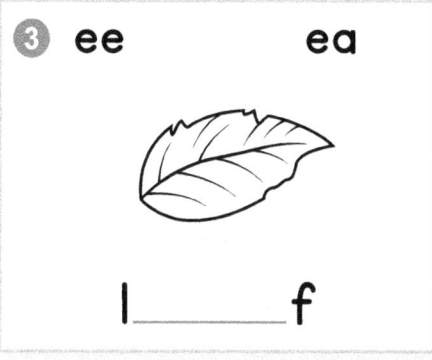
l_____f

4. au   aw

f_____cet

5. oo   ow

fl_____er

6. oa   ow
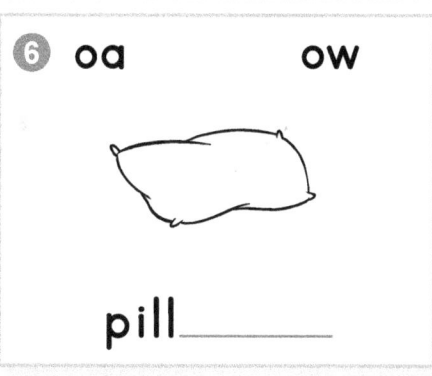
pill_____

7. er   ir

tig_____

8. ea   ee
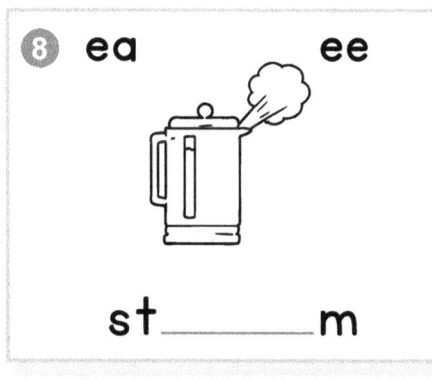
st_____m

9. ar   or

f_____k

10. oa   ow

sn_____

11. au   aw

_____tumn

12. er   ur

t_____tle

Vowel Pairs Review

Say the name of the object out loud.
Fill in the missing vowel pair for the word.

① ee   ea

sh___p

② oa   ow

cl___n

③ er   ur

hamm___

④ oa   ow

b___t

⑤ ar   or

sh___k

⑥ oa   ow

___l

⑦ oa   ow

c___t

⑧ ir   ur
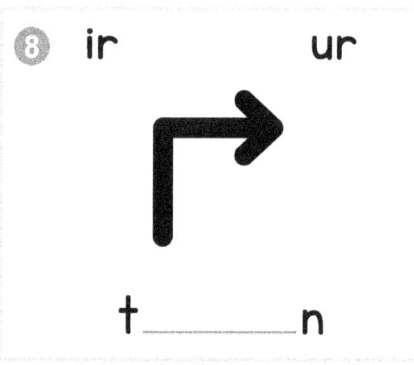
t___n

⑨ ew   ui
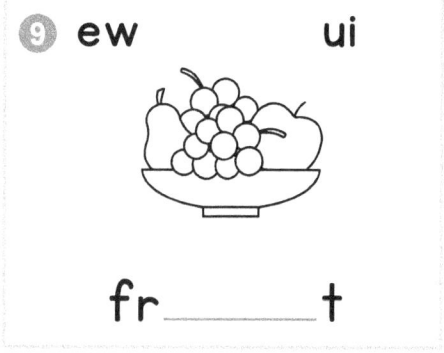
fr___t

⑩ ar   or

b___n

⑪ oi   oy

b___

⑫ ee   ea
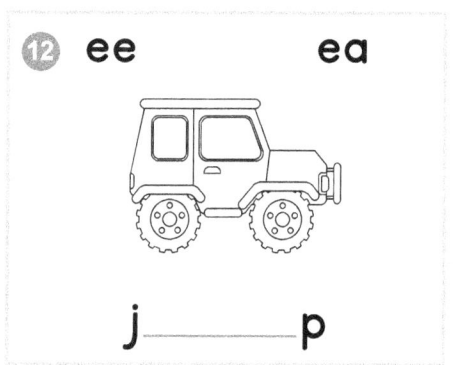
j___p

Vowel Pairs Review

Say the name of the object out loud.
Fill in the missing vowel pair for the word.

① oa   ow

b____l

② ar   or
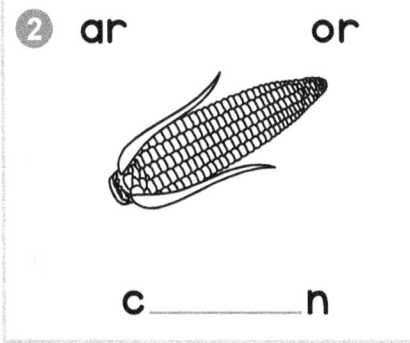
c____n

③ er   ur

b____n

④ oa   ou

m____se

⑤ au   aw

p____

⑥ oi   oy
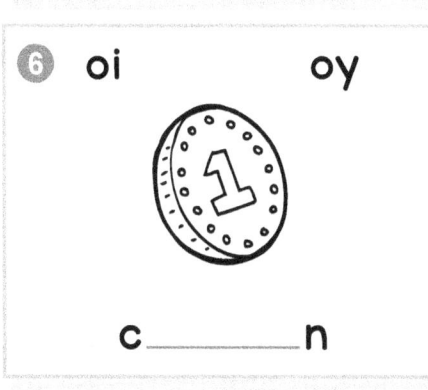
c____n

⑦ ee   ea

tr____

⑧ ir   er
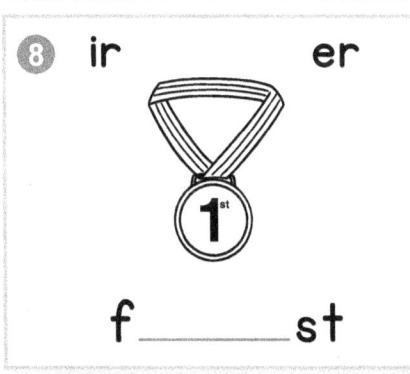
f____st

⑨ ew   ui
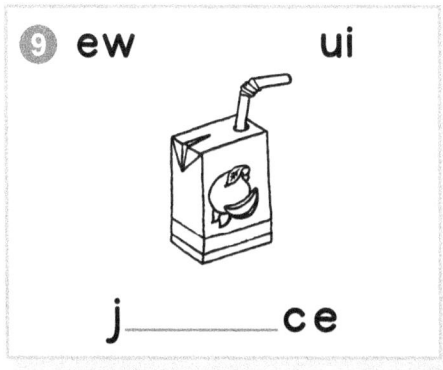
j____ce

⑩ oa   ow

fl____er

⑪ oa   ow

g____t

⑫ ee   ea
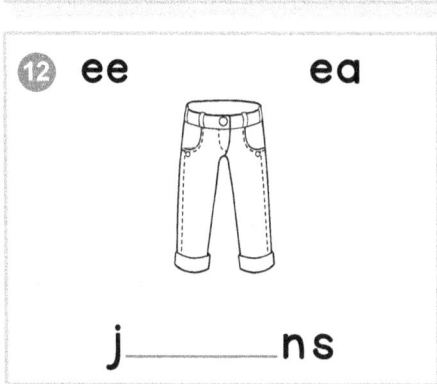
j____ns

Word Families

Word Family: ack

Write a silly story using as many words as you can from the word family.

| attack | back | crack | Jack |
| lack | pack | snack | track |

☐ I used capitals and end marks.   ☐ My printing is neat.   ☐ My writing makes sense.

Word Family: ail

Write a silly story using as many words as you can from the word family.

| fail | hail | jail | mail |
| nail | sail | snail | tail |

_____

_____

_____

_____

_____

☐ I used capitals and end marks. ☐ My printing is neat. ☐ My writing makes sense.

Word Family: ain

Write a silly story using as many words as you can from the word family.

brain	chain	gain	main
pain	rain	stain	train

☐ I used capitals and end marks. ☐ My printing is neat. ☐ My writing makes sense.

Word Family: ake

Write a silly story using as many words as you can from the word family.

awake	bake	cake	flake
lake	make	snake	take

_____

_____

_____

_____

_____

☐ I used capitals and end marks. ☐ My printing is neat. ☐ My writing makes sense.

Word Family: all

Write a silly story using as many words as you can from the word family.

all	ball	call	fall
hall	mall	small	tall

_____

_____

_____

_____

_____

_____

☐ I used capitals and end marks. ☐ My printing is neat. ☐ My writing makes sense.

Word Family: ame

Write a silly story using as many words as you can from the word family.

| came | fame | flame | frame |
| game | lame | name | same |

☐ I used capitals and end marks. ☐ My printing is neat. ☐ My writing makes sense.

Word Family: ash

Write a silly story using as many words as you can from the word family.

| ash | bash | cash | crash |
| dash | flash | rash | splash |

_____

_____

_____

_____

_____

☐ I used capitals and end marks. ☐ My printing is neat. ☐ My writing makes sense.

Word Family: eat

Write a silly story using as many words as you can from the word family.

| cheat | eat | repeat | heat |
| meat | neat | treat | wheat |

☐ I used capitals and end marks.   ☐ My printing is neat.   ☐ My writing makes sense.

Word Family: eep

Write a silly story using as many words as you can from the word family.

| beep | deep | jeep | keep |
| sheep | sleep | steep | sweep |

☐ I used capitals and end marks. ☐ My printing is neat. ☐ My writing makes sense.

Word Family: ell

Write a silly story using as many words as you can from the word family.

| bell | fell | sell | shell |
| smell | spell | tell | yell |

_____
_____
_____
_____
_____
_____

☐ I used capitals and end marks.   ☐ My printing is neat.   ☐ My writing makes sense.

Word Family: ice

Write a silly story using as many words as you can from the word family.

dice	ice	mice	nice
price	slice	spice	twice

_____

_____

_____

_____

_____

_____

☐ I used capitals and end marks. ☐ My printing is neat. ☐ My writing makes sense.

Word Family: ide

Write a silly story using as many words as you can from the word family.

bride	decide	glide	hide
pride	ride	side	wide

_____

_____

_____

_____

_____

☐ I used capitals and end marks.   ☐ My printing is neat.   ☐ My writing makes sense.

Word Family: ight

Write a silly story using as many words as you can from the word family.

| bright | fight | flight | height |
| knight | light | might | right |

☐ I used capitals and end marks. ☐ My printing is neat. ☐ My writing makes sense.

Word Family: ing

Write a silly story using as many words as you can from the word family.

bring	king	ring	sing
spring	sting	thing	wing

_____

_____

_____

_____

_____

☐ I used capitals and end marks.   ☐ My printing is neat.   ☐ My writing makes sense.

Word Family: ink

Write a silly story using as many words as you can from the word family.

| blink | drink | rink | shrink |
| sink | stink | think | wink |

☐ I used capitals and end marks. ☐ My printing is neat. ☐ My writing makes sense.

Word Family: oat

Write a silly story using as many words as you can from the word family.

boat	coat	float	gloat
goat	oat	throat	

_____

_____

_____

_____

_____

☐ I used capitals and end marks. ☐ My printing is neat. ☐ My writing makes sense.

Word Family: ock

Write a silly story using as many words as you can from the word family.

| block | clock | dock | flock |
| knock | lock | rock | sock |

_____
_____
_____
_____
_____
_____

☐ I used capitals and end marks.   ☐ My printing is neat.   ☐ My writing makes sense.

Word Family: op

Write a silly story using as many words as you can from the word family.

| bop | chop | cop | drop |
| hop | mop | flop | shop |

_____

_____

_____

_____

_____

☐ I used capitals and end marks.   ☐ My printing is neat.   ☐ My writing makes sense.

Word Family: own

Write a silly story using as many words as you can from the word family.

| brown | clown | crown | down |
| drown | frown | gown | town |

_____

_____

_____

_____

_____

☐ I used capitals and end marks.   ☐ My printing is neat.   ☐ My writing makes sense.

Word Family: uck

Write a silly story using as many words as you can from the word family.

buck	cluck	luck	muck
stuck	truck	tuck	yuck

_____

_____

_____

_____

_____

☐ I used capitals and end marks.   ☐ My printing is neat.   ☐ My writing makes sense.

Word Family: ump

Write a silly story using as many words as you can from the word family.

| bump | clump | dump | jump |
| lump | pump | stump | thump |

_____

_____

_____

_____

_____

_____

☐ I used capitals and end marks.   ☐ My printing is neat.   ☐ My writing makes sense.

Word Family: ug

Write a silly story using as many words as you can from the word family.

bug	dug	jug	mug
plug	pug	rug	snug

_____

_____

_____

_____

_____

_____

☐ I used capitals and end marks.   ☐ My printing is neat.   ☐ My writing makes sense.

Word Family: unk

Write a silly story using as many words as you can from the word family.

| bunk | chunk | Chipmunk | junk |
| plunk | skunk | sunk | trunk |

___

☐ I used capitals and end marks. ☐ My printing is neat. ☐ My writing makes sense.

More Activities

Phonics Practice Menu

Colour Code	Rainbow Words	Hidden Words
Write out a word family using one colour for the vowels and another colour for the consonants.	Write out a word family into the shape of a rainbow using the colours of the rainbow.	Draw a picture outline. Add a word family to the picture so they are "hiding." Colour your picture.
Cut It Out!	**Word Search**	**Rhyming Words**
Cut letters out of a magazine. Spell out a word family and glue them onto a sheet of paper.	Create a word search based on a word family.	Write out a word family with a rhyming word next to each word.
Alphabetical Order	**Spelling Word Typing**	**Magnetic Letter Words**
Print a word family in alphabetical order.	Type a word family on a computer or other device.	Use magnetic letters to make a word family.
Spelling Race	**Sort It Out**	**Spelling Word Fun**
How many times can you write out a word family in three minutes?	Sort a word family into categories of your choice and record them on a piece of paper.	Form a word family using • modelling clay • pipe cleaners • toothpicks

_____ **Rainbow Word Family**

> Pick a word family. Say each word out loud.
> Copy and spell each word three times using colours of your choice.

's Word Search

_____'s Tongue Twisters

Write a tongue twister based on a word family.

Word Family: _____

_____

_____

Word Family: _____

_____

_____

Word Family: _____

_____

_____

A Web About...

_____

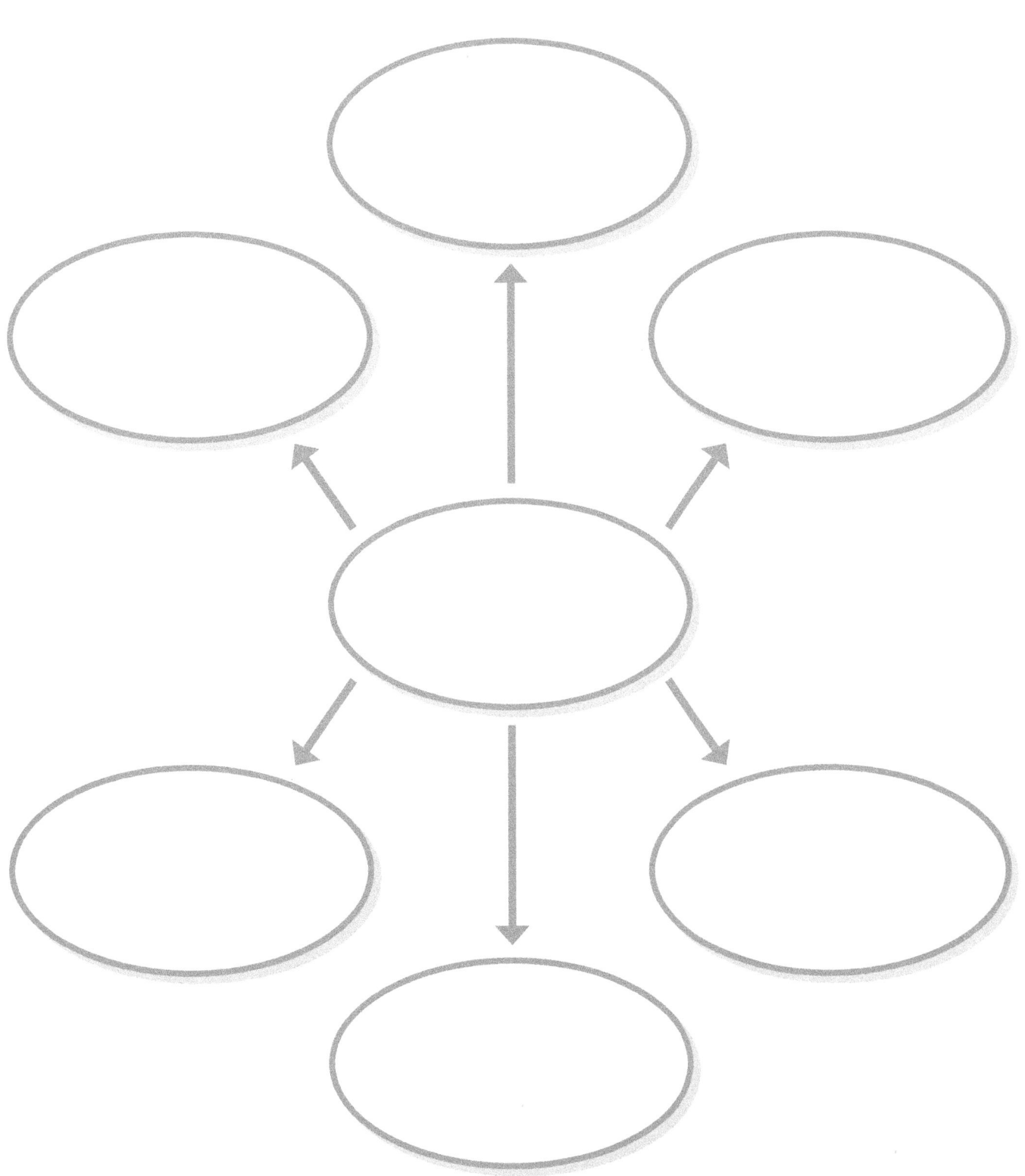

Practice Page

How am I Doing?

	Completing my work	Using my time wisely	Following directions	Keeping organized
Full Speed Ahead!	• My work is always complete and done with care. • I added extra details to my work.	• I always get my work done on time.	• I always follow directions.	• My materials are always neatly organized. • I am always prepared and ready to learn.
Keep Going!	• My work is complete and done with care. • I added extra details to my work.	• I usually get my work done on time.	• I usually follow directions without reminders.	• I usually can find my materials. • I am usually prepared and ready to learn.
Slow Down!	• My work is complete. • I need to check my work.	• I sometimes get my work done on time.	• I sometimes need reminders to follow directions.	• I sometimes need time to find my materials. • I am sometimes prepared and ready to learn.
Stop!	• My work is not complete. • I need to check my work.	• I rarely get my work done on time.	• I need reminders to follow directions.	• I need to organize my materials. • I am rarely prepared and ready to learn.

I am proud of…

I will work on…

Reading Strategies

Eagle Eye

Look at the picture.

What is in the picture that starts with the beginning sound?

Lips the Fish

Get your mouth ready!

Say the beginning sound right away.

Chunky Monkey

Break the word into chunks and small words you know!

B <u>ag</u>   Fl <u>ag</u>

Re-Tryin' Lion

Re-read the sentence.

Think, "What makes sense?"

Reading Strategies

Stretchy Snake

Slowly stretch each letter sound to read the word.

s - t - r - e - t - c - h

Skippy Squirrel

Skip the tricky words. Read to the end.

Go back and try to re-read the words.

Flippy Dolphin

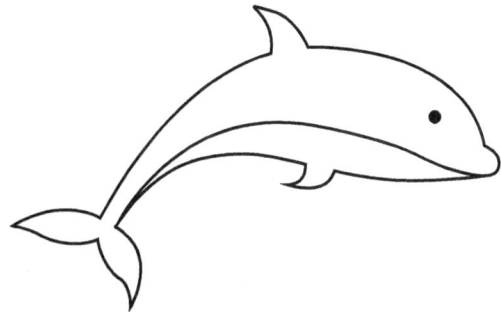

Flip the vowel sounds. If the short vowel sound does not work try the long vowel sound.

Careful Chameleon

Carefully read the whole word. Think about the word parts.

Think, *"What makes sense?"*

Answers

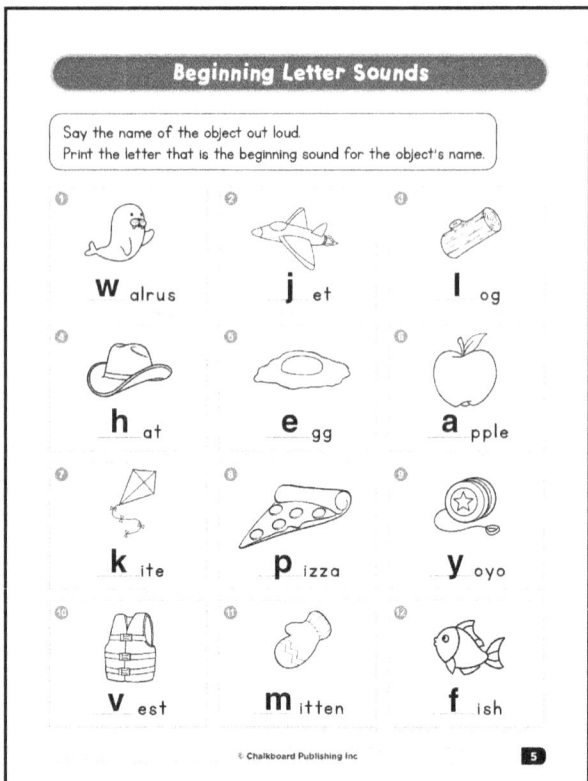
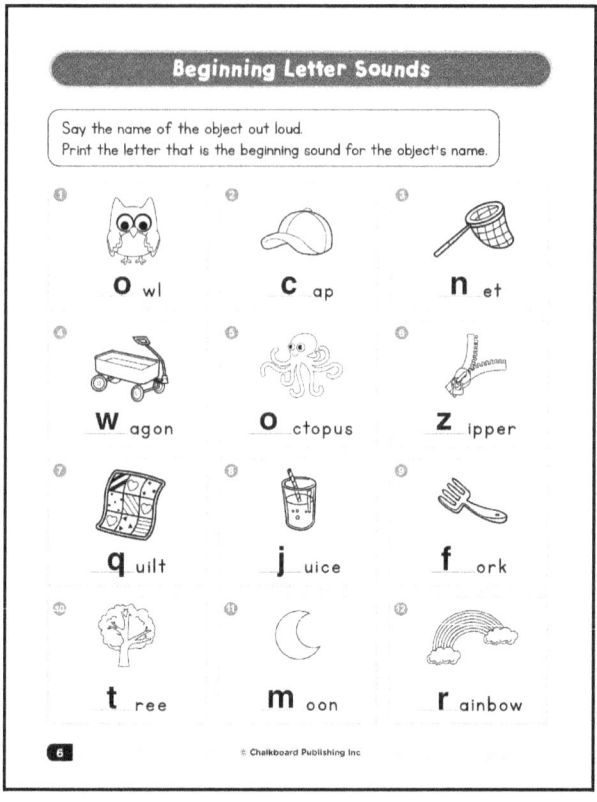

Answers

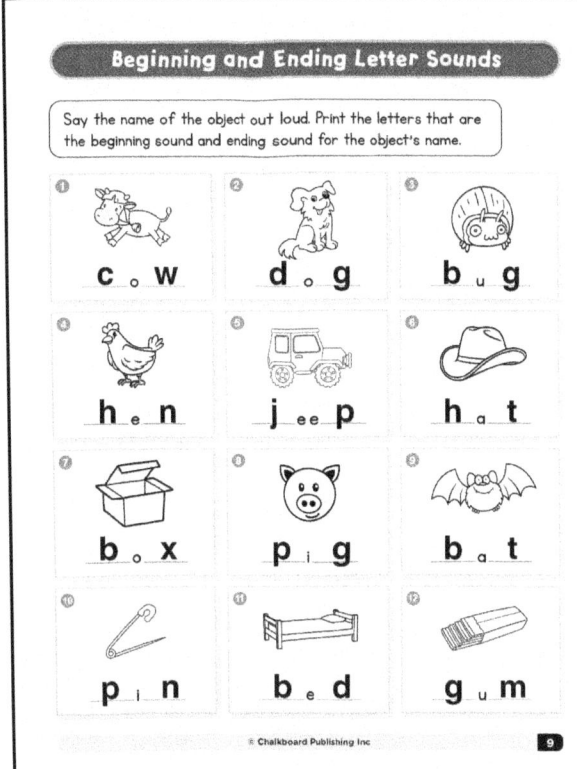
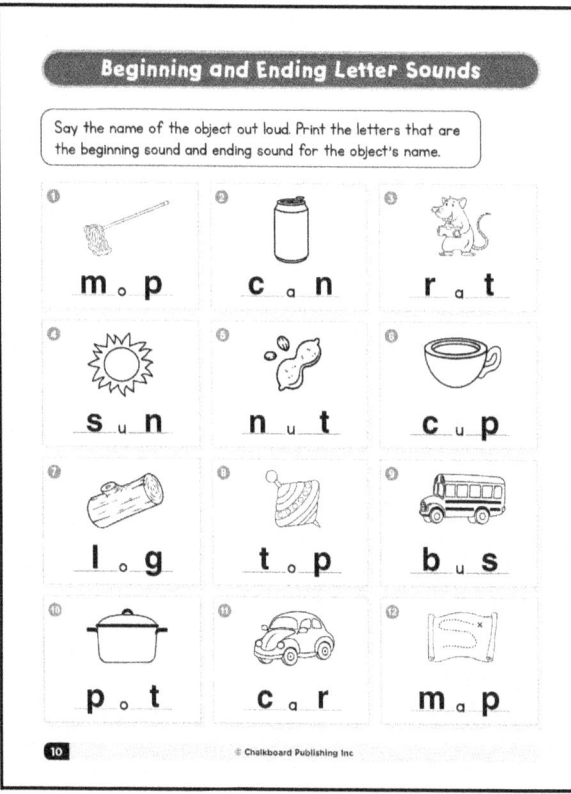
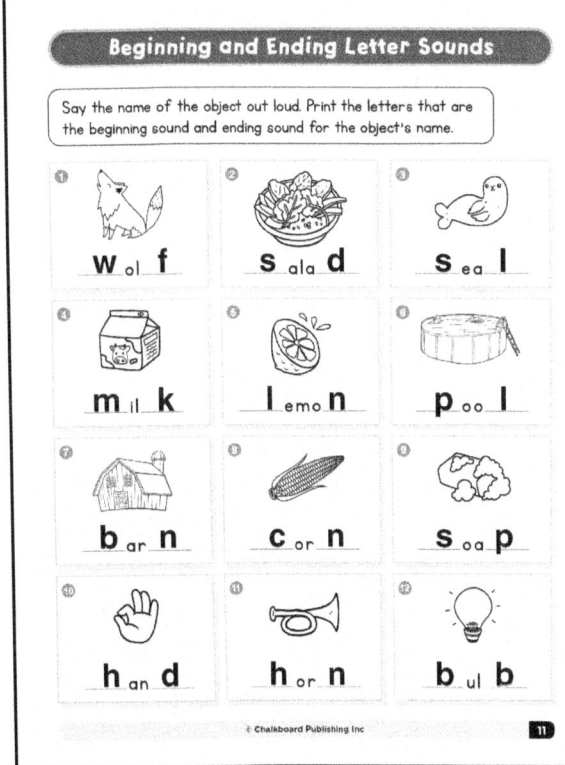
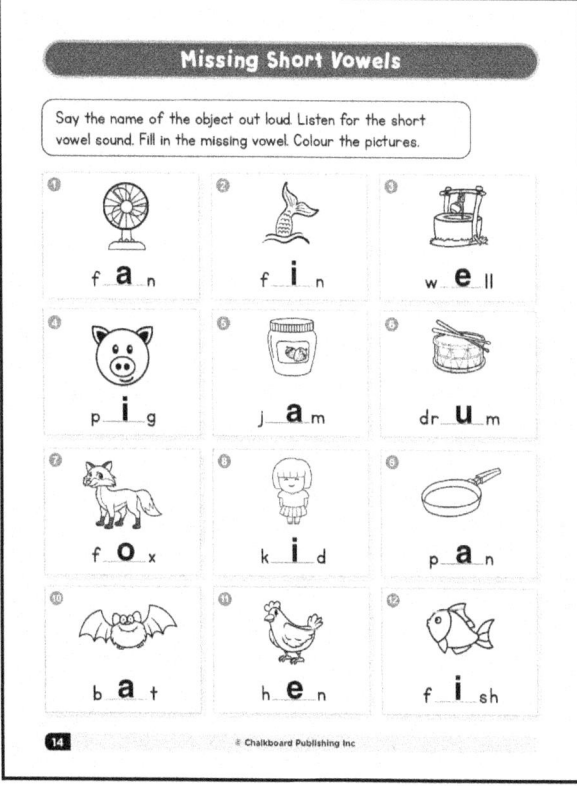

Answers

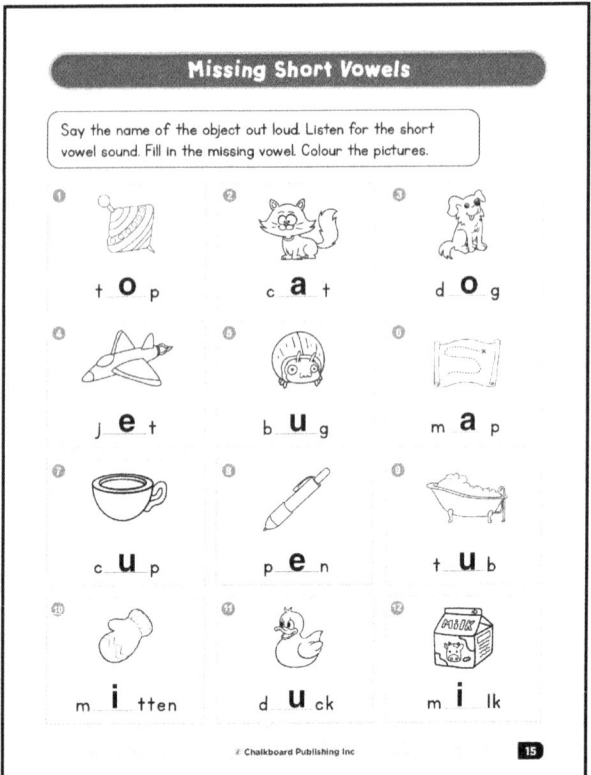
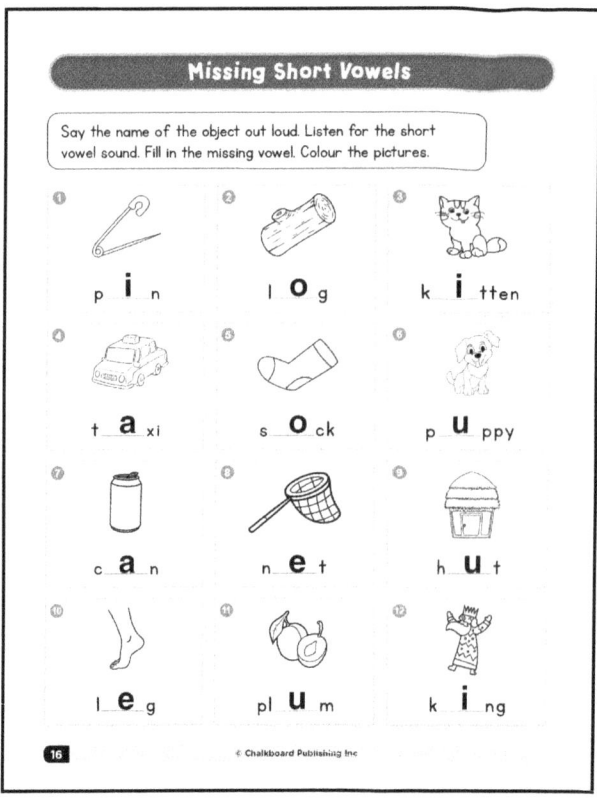
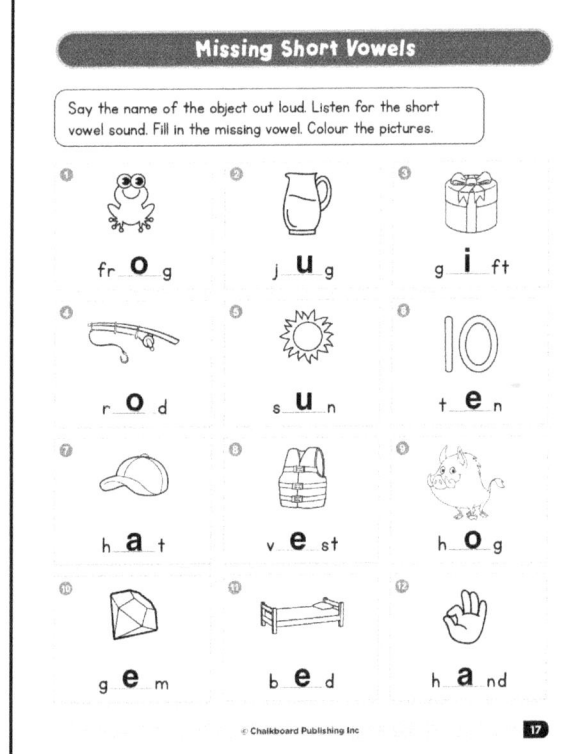

Answers

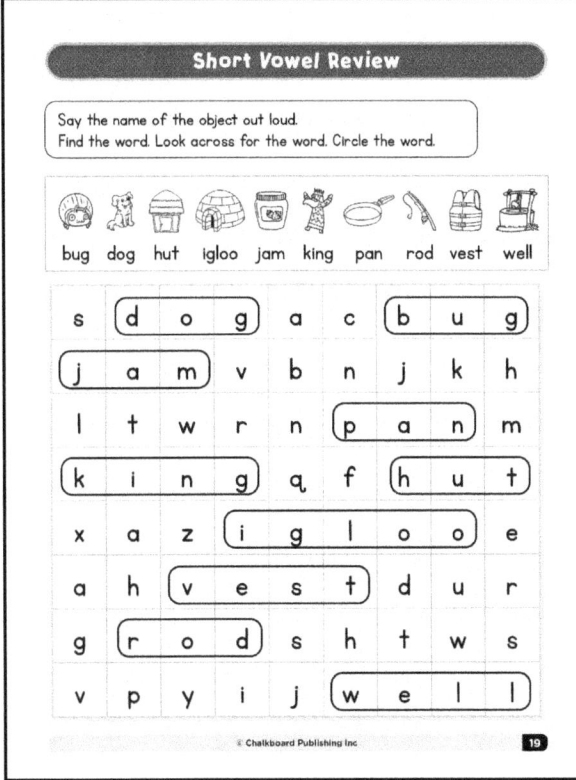

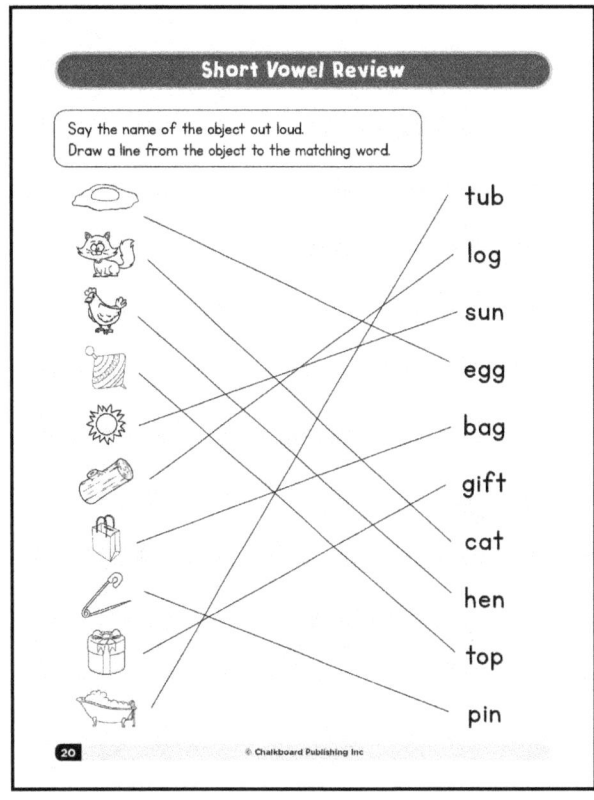

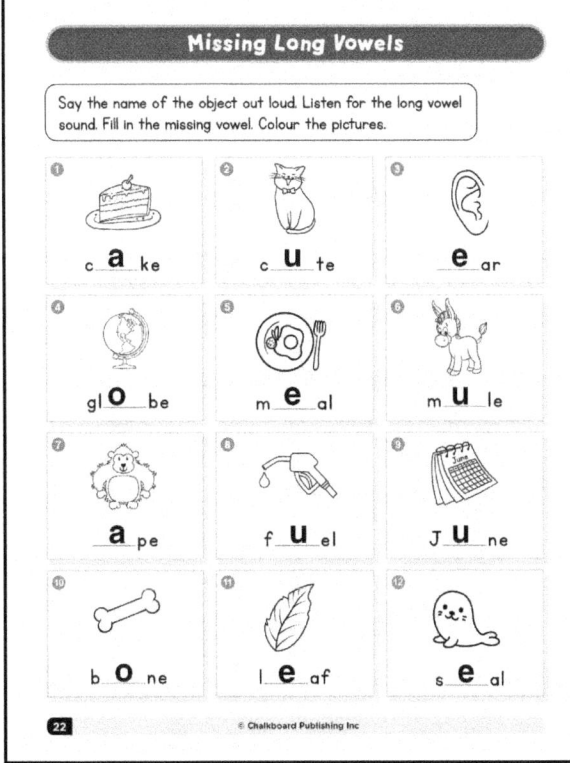

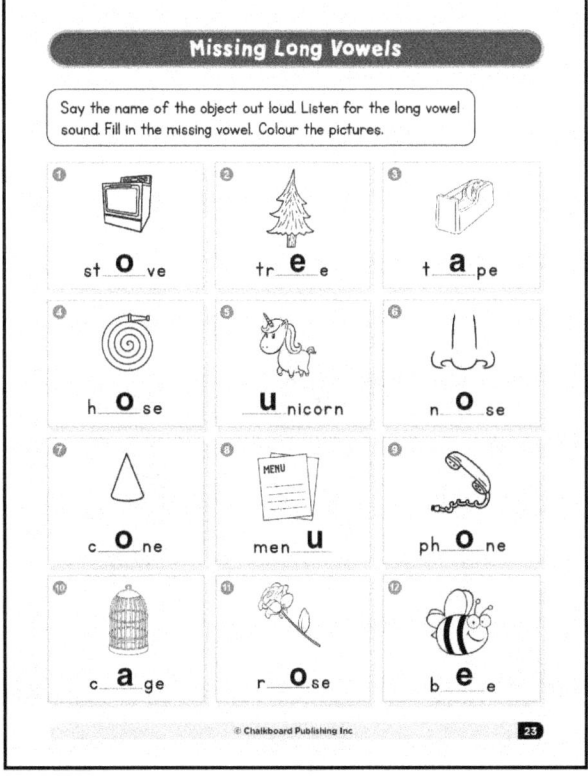

Answers

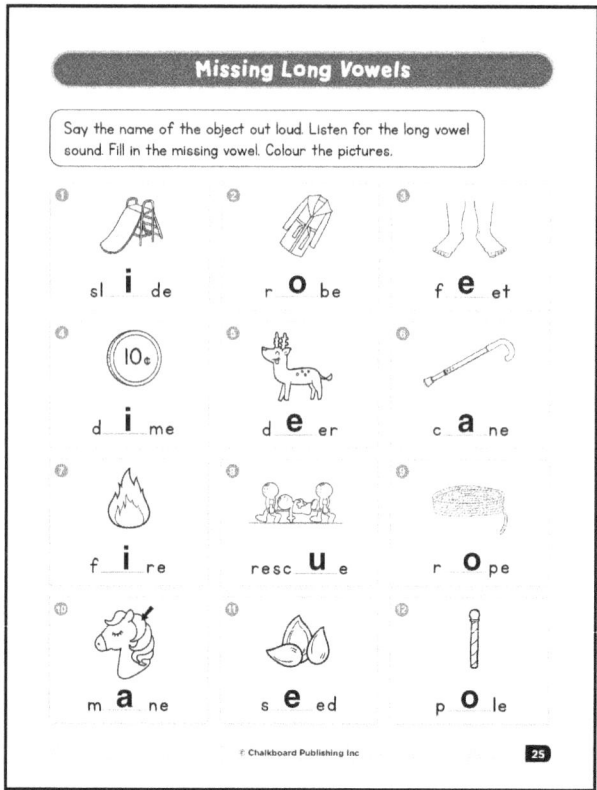

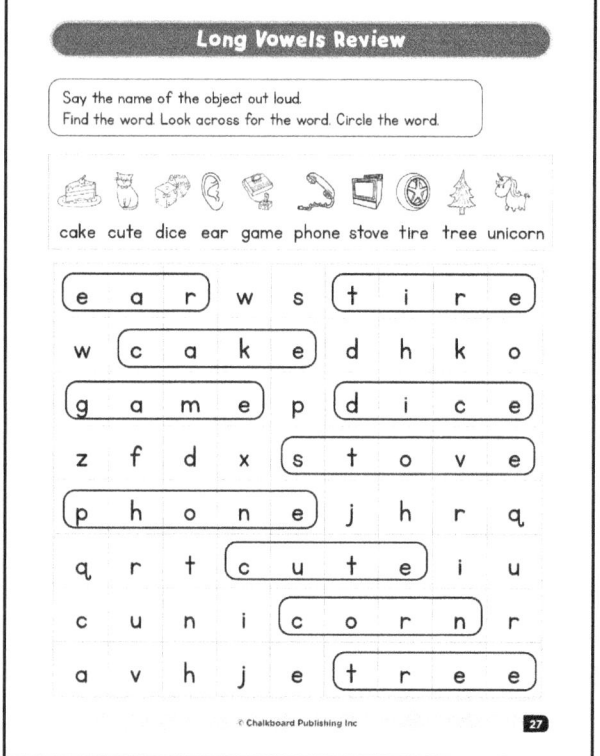

Answers

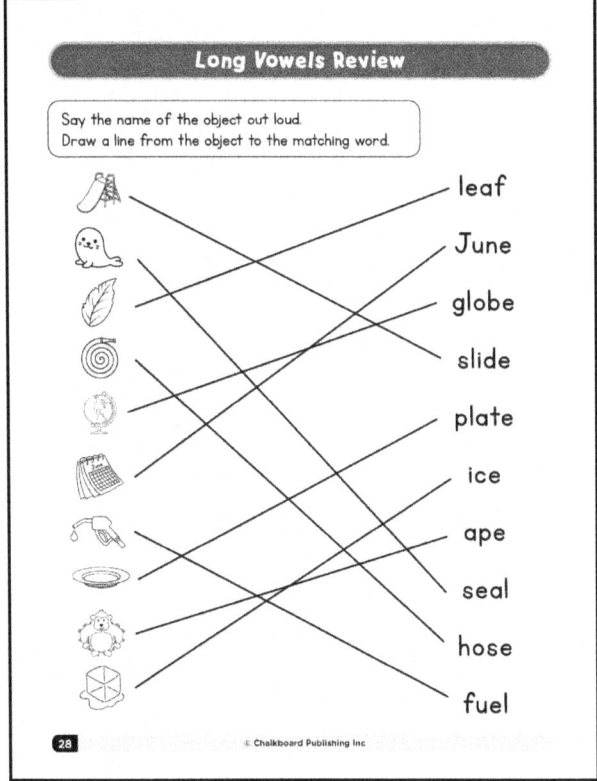

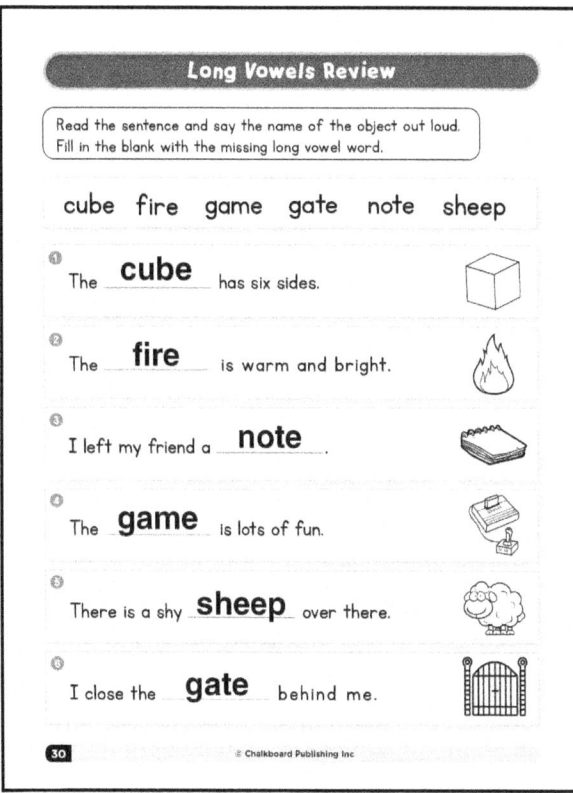

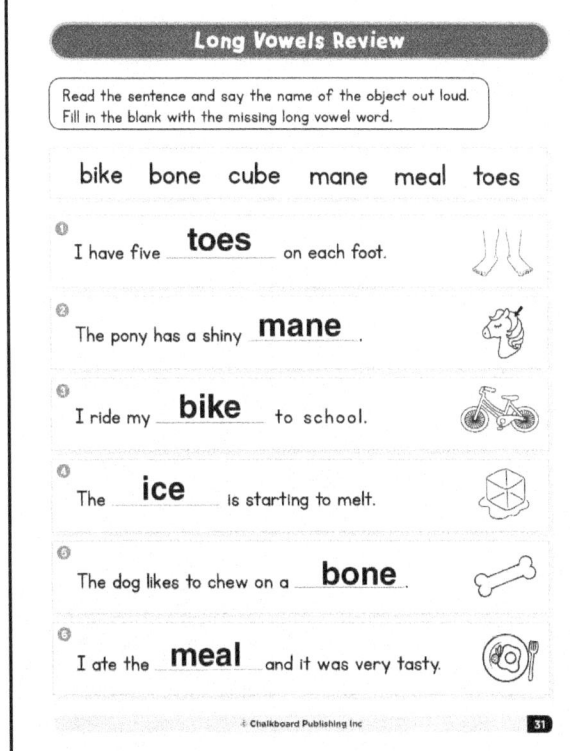

Answers

Short and Long Vowels Review

Read the sentence.
Fill in the blank with the correct word for each sentence.

1. I **ate** a sandwich for lunch today. — at / ate
2. I **hope** the weather is sunny. — hop / hope
3. I picked up the **tube** of toothpaste. — tub / tube
4. My dad is wearing a red **cap** on his head. — cap / cape
5. I will get my hair **cut** today. — cut / cute
6. I am **mad** at my friend. — mad / made
7. I **can** do a handstand! — can / cane

Short and Long Vowels Review

Read the sentence.
Fill in the blank with the correct word for each sentence.

1. My grandpa uses a **cane** to walk. — can / cane
2. The kitten is small and very **cute**. — cut / cute
3. My parents **made** me clean my room. — mad / made
4. The little bunny can **hop** very high! — hop / hope
5. A superhero wears a long **cape**. — cap / cape
6. The **tub** is ready for my bubble bath. — tub / tube
7. There are many kids **at** school. — at / ate

Short and Long Vowels Review

Say the name of the object out loud. Draw a line from the object to the matching word. Colour the pictures.

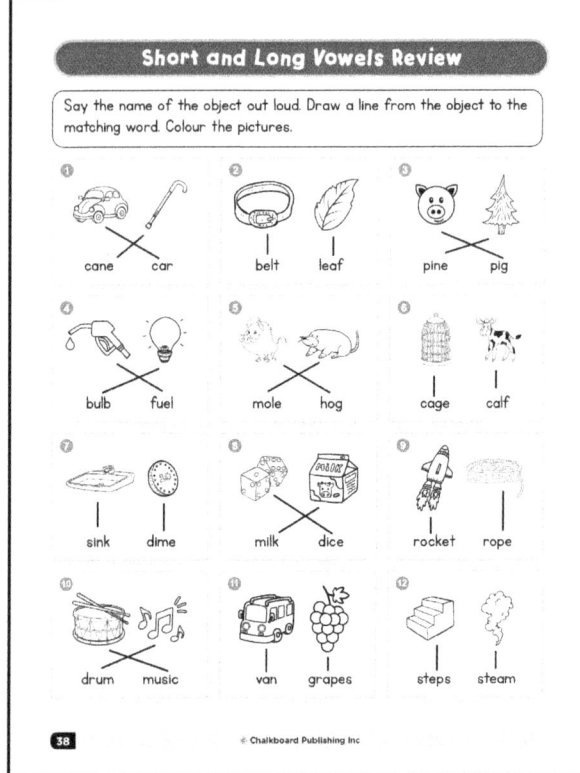

Short and Long Vowels Review

Say the name of the object out loud. Draw a line from the object to the matching word. Colour the pictures.

Answers

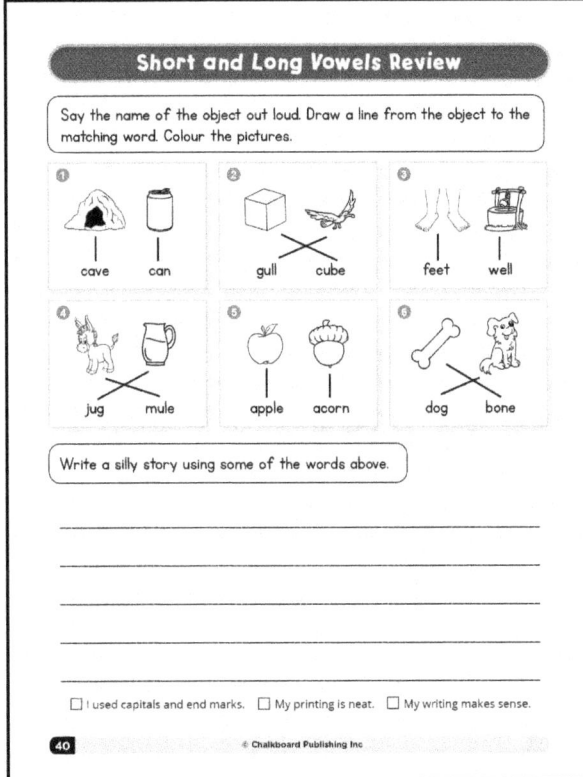

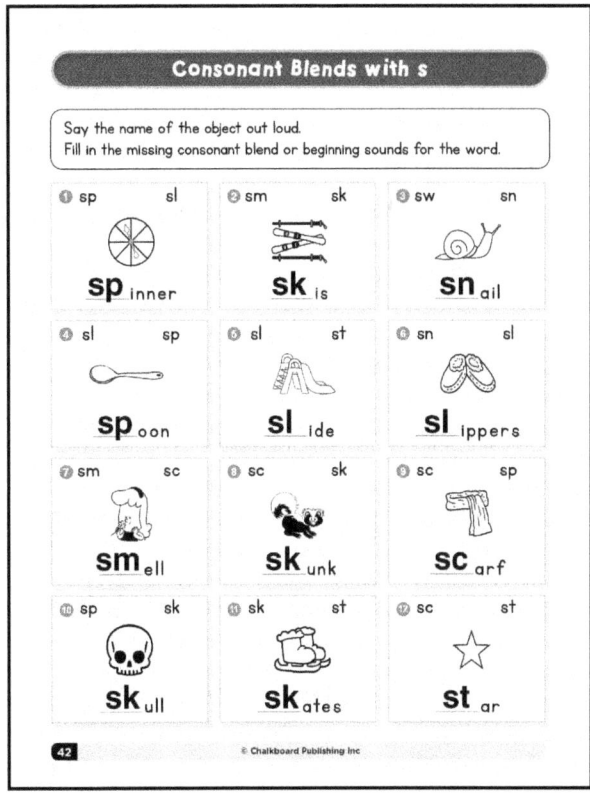

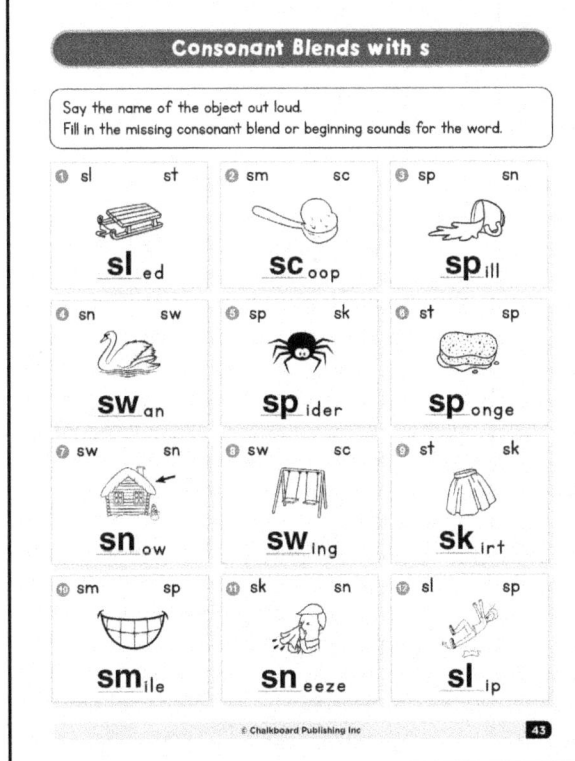

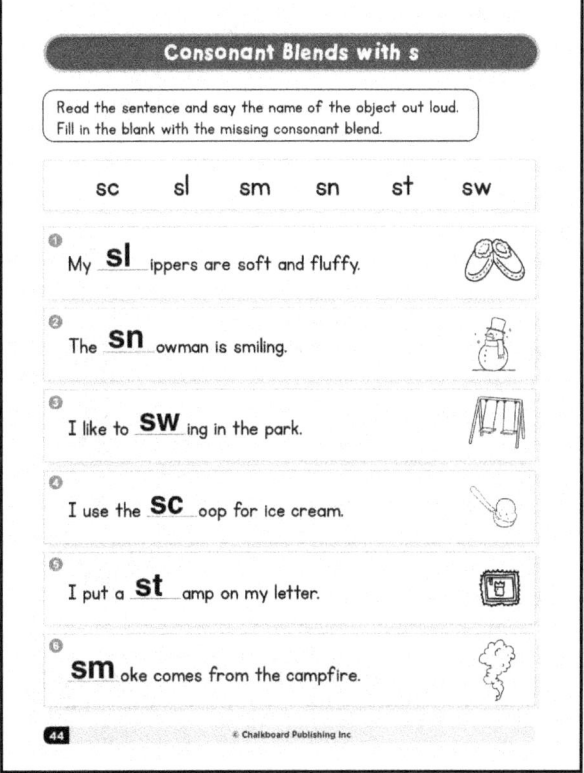

Answers

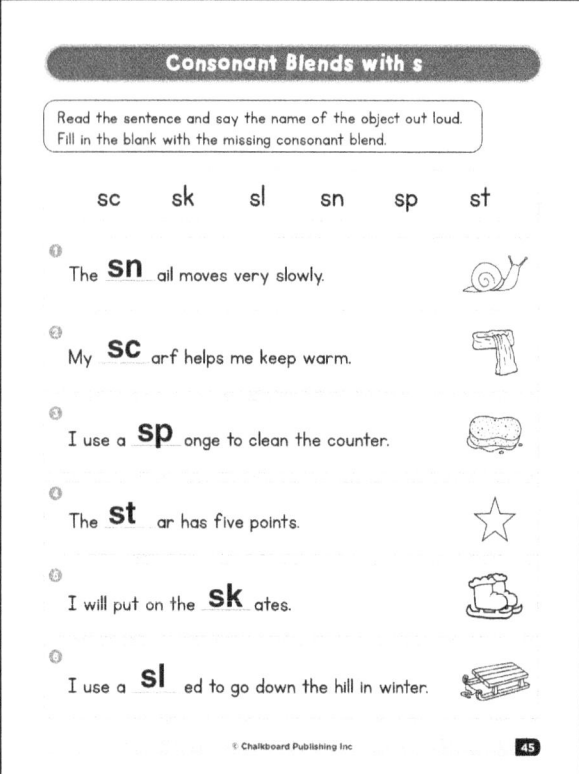
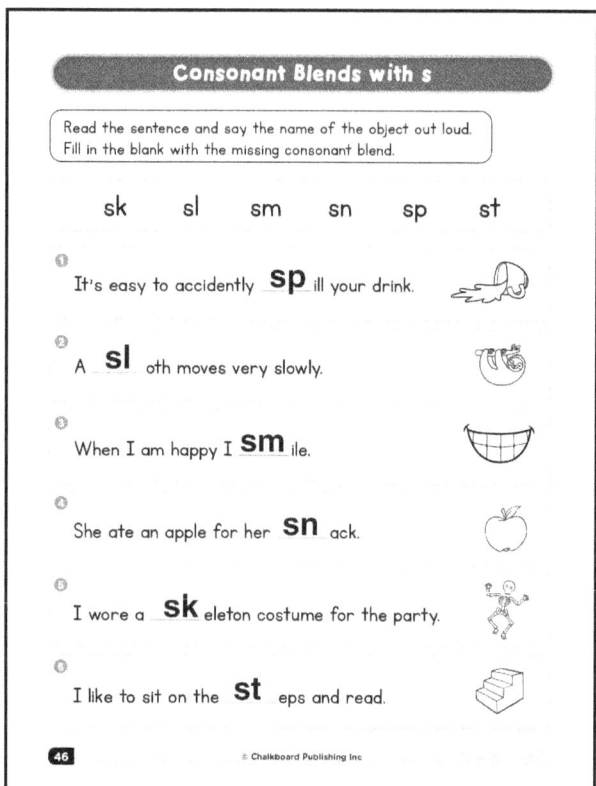
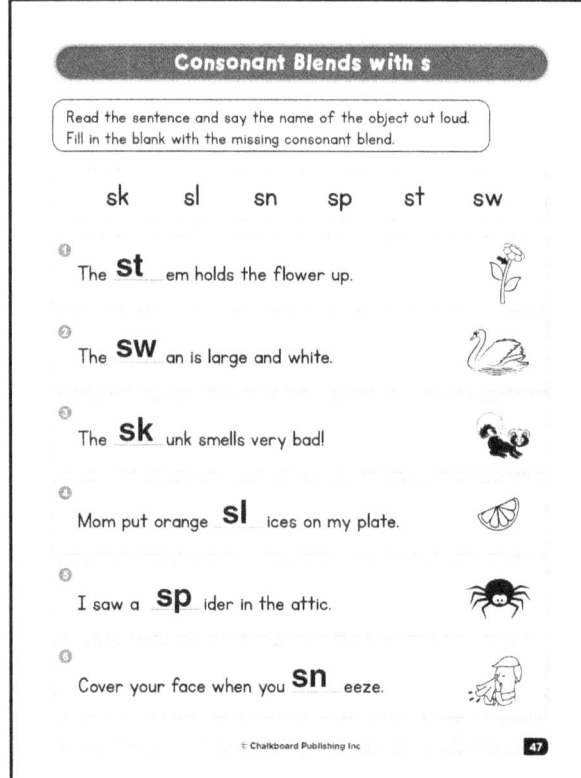
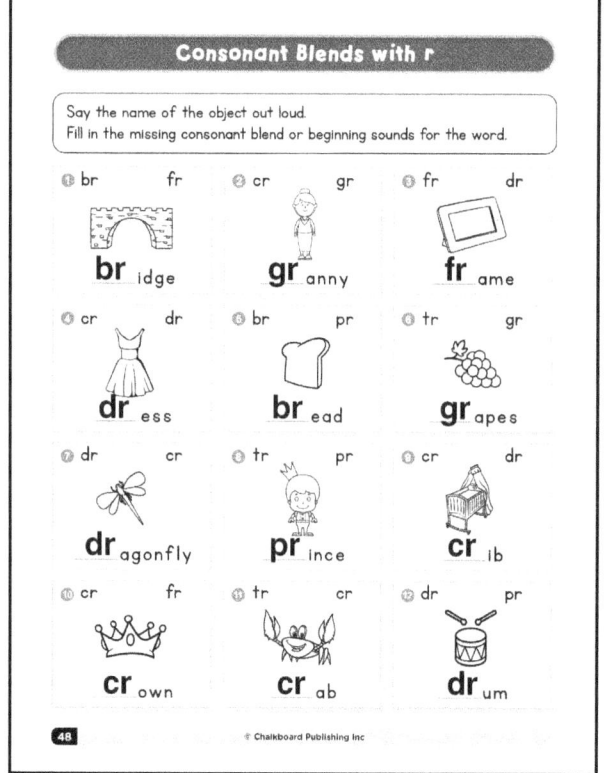

Answers

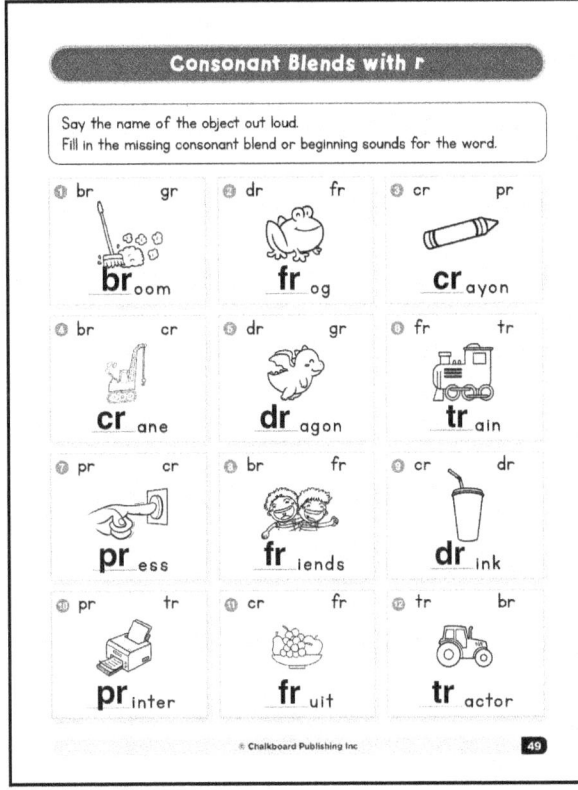

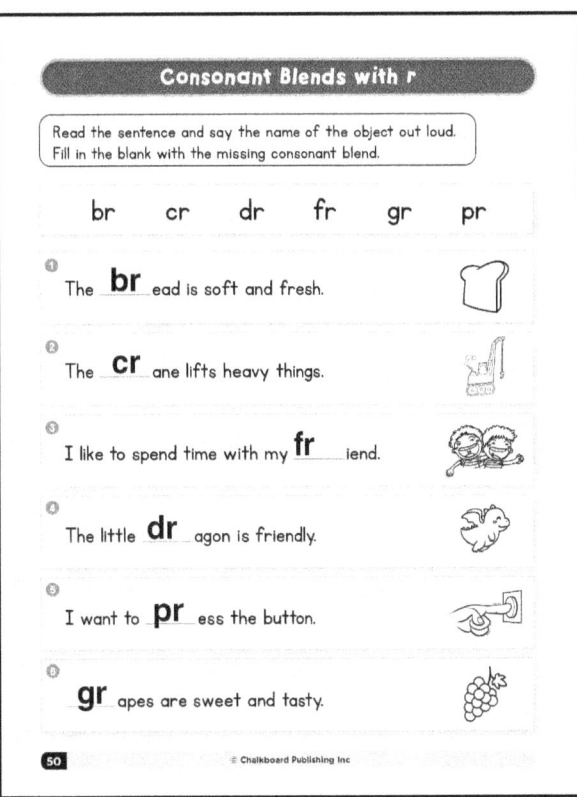

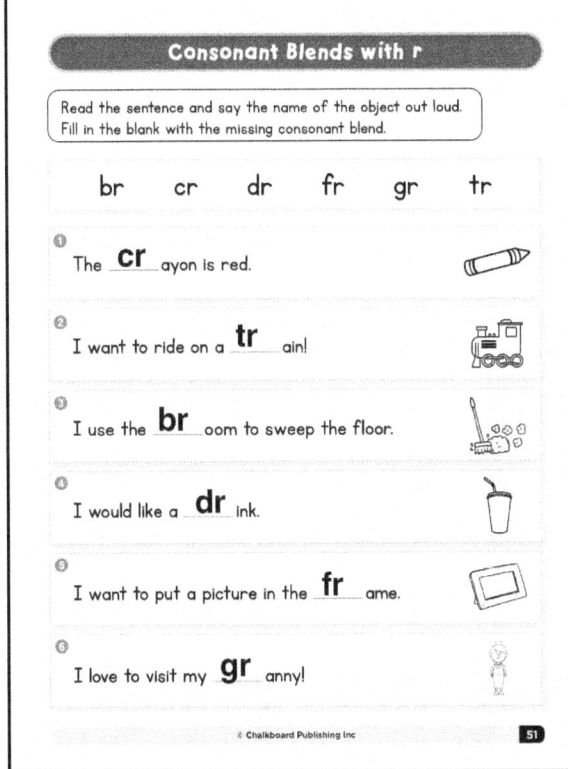

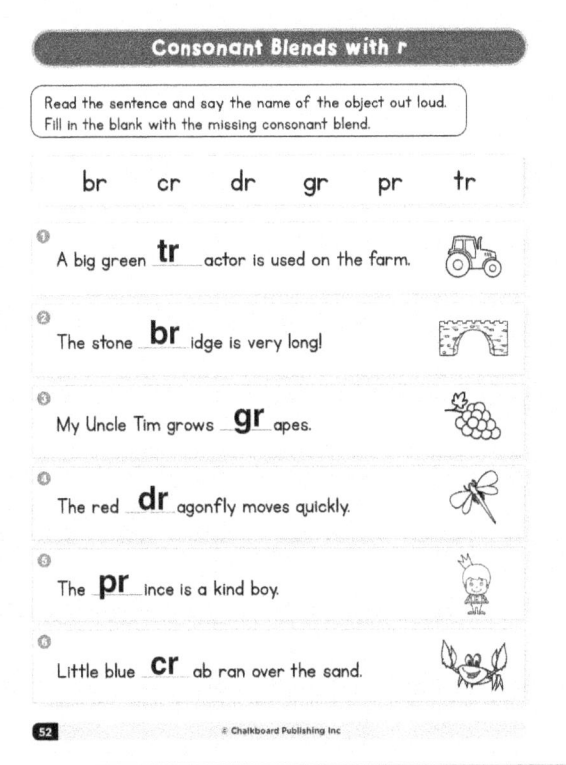

Answers

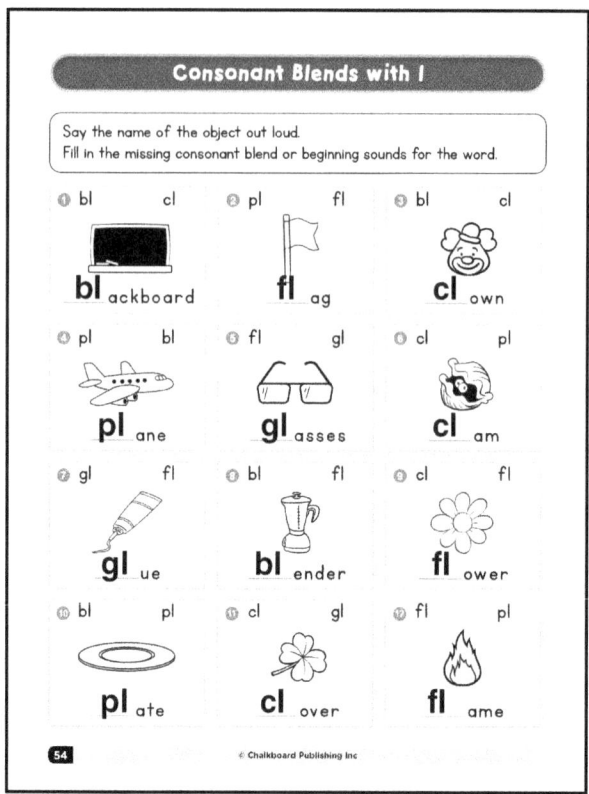
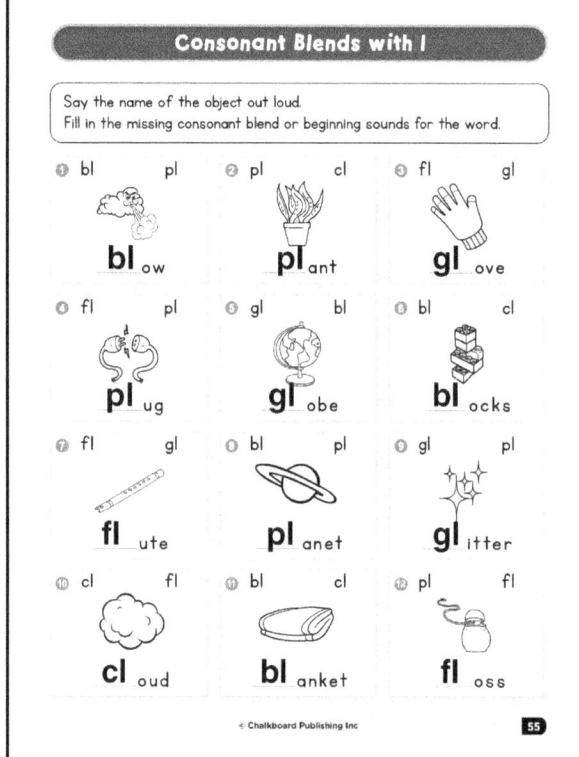
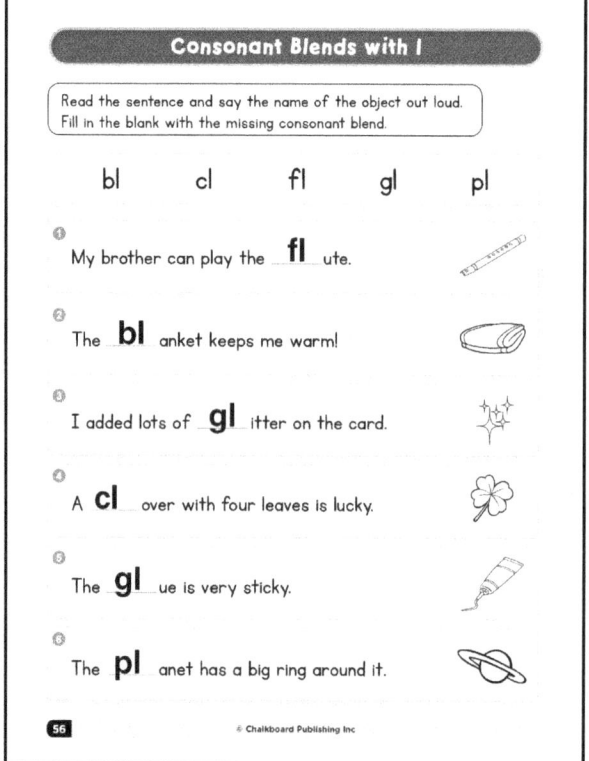

Answers

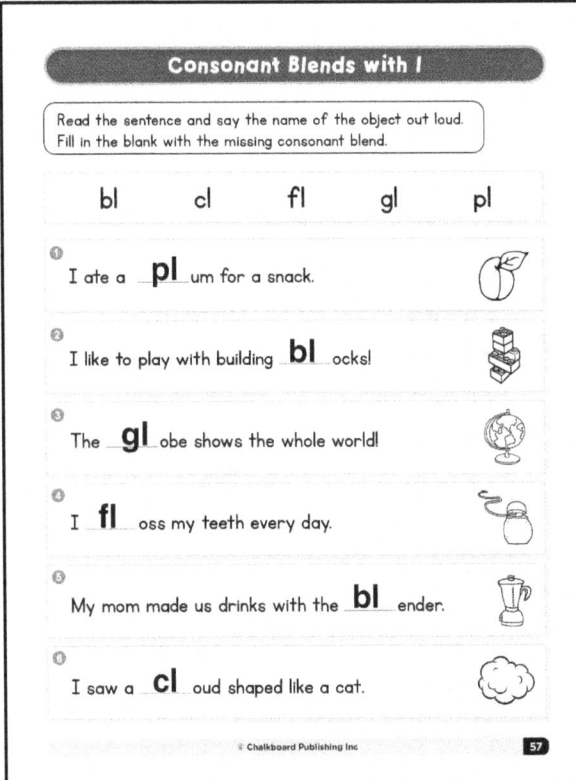

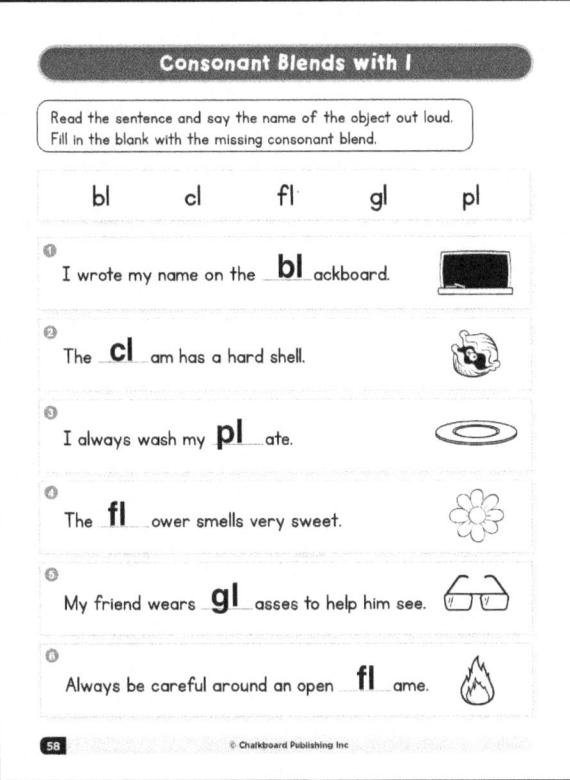

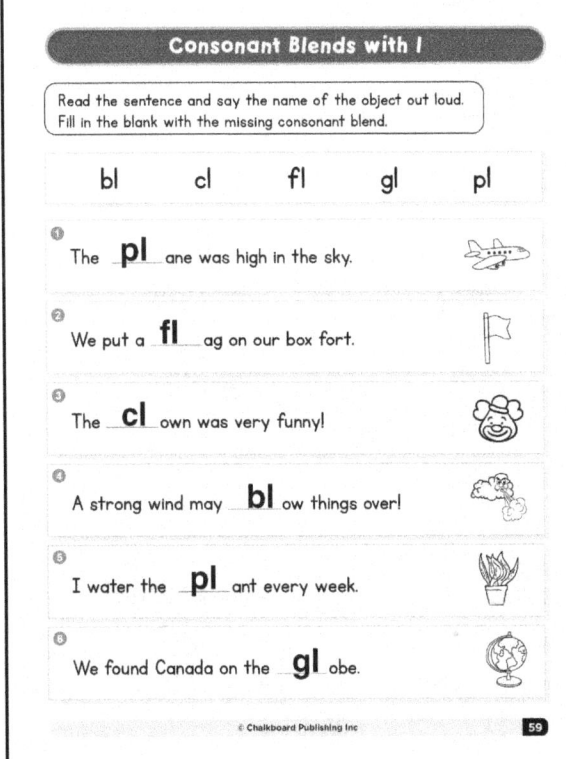

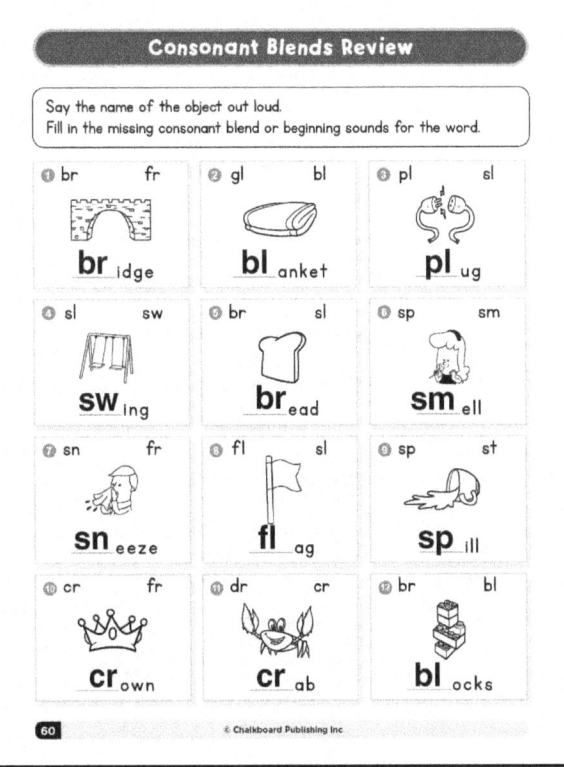

Answers

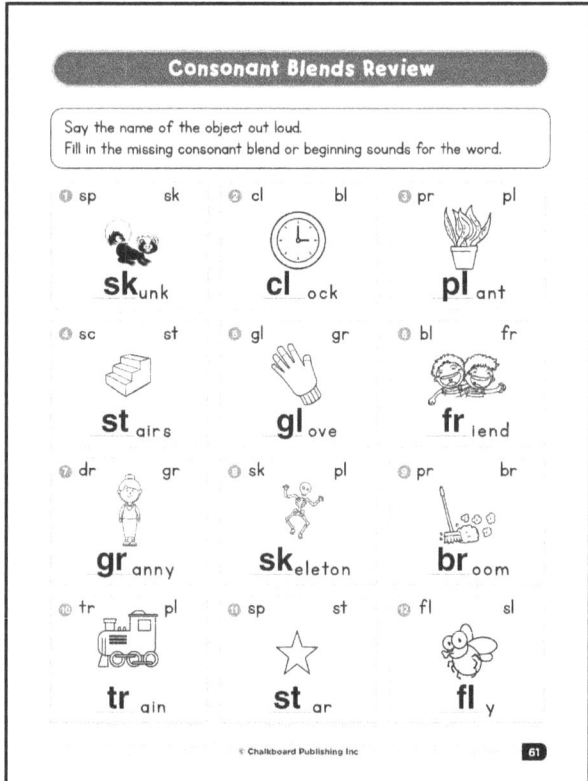

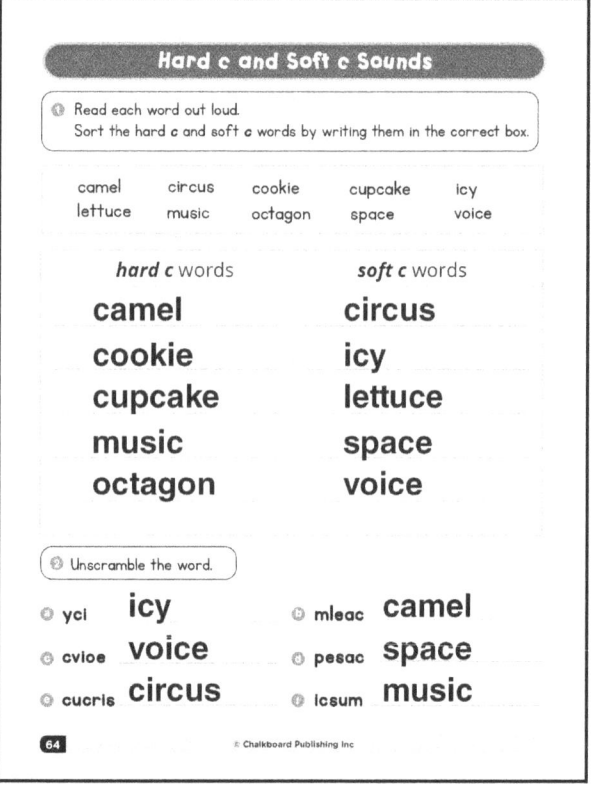

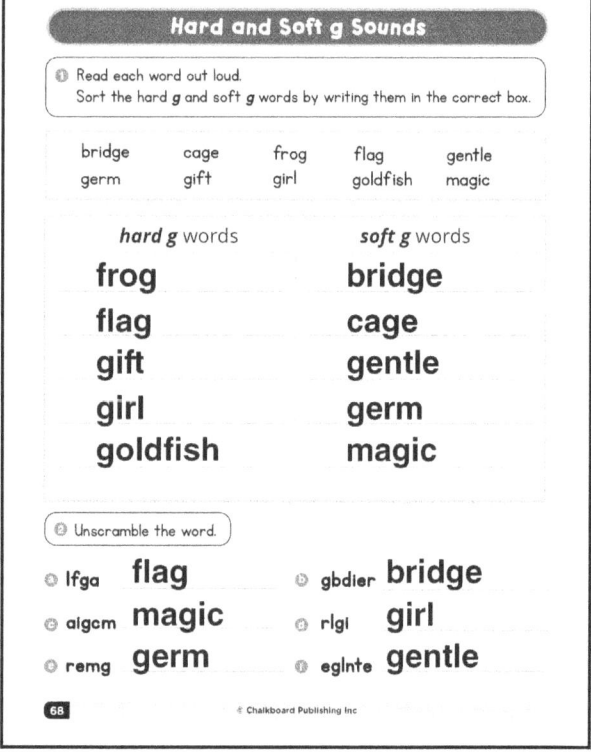

Answers

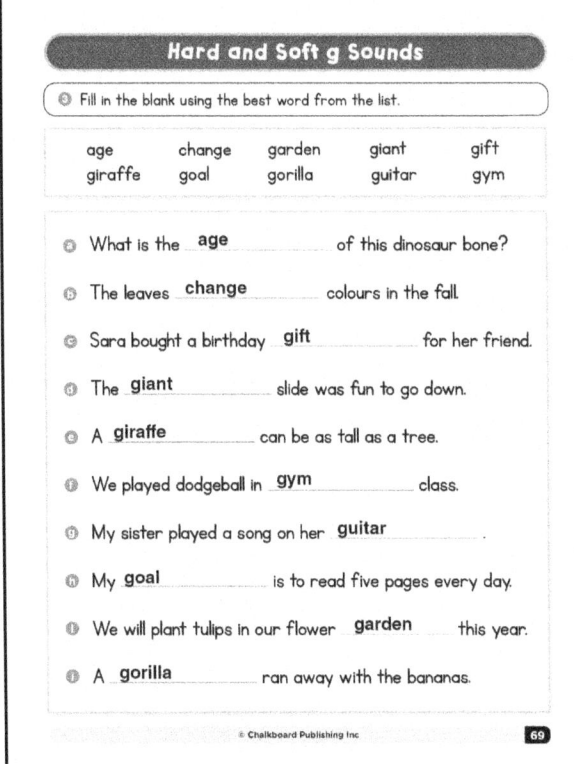

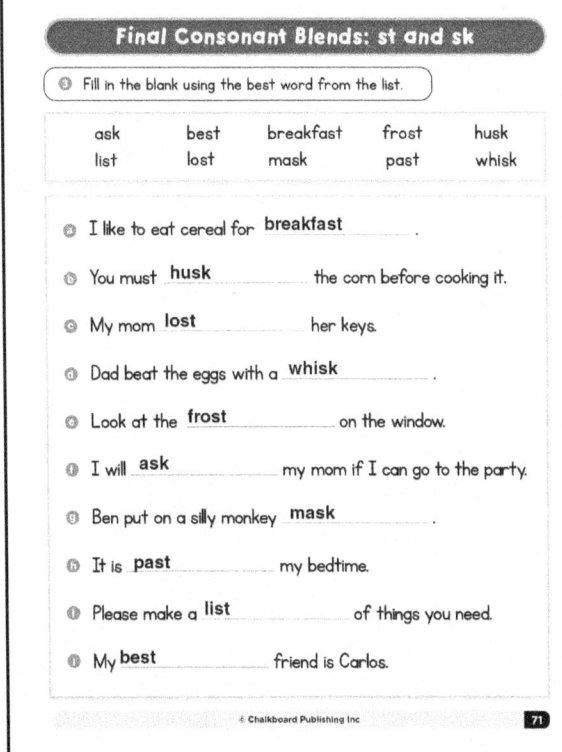
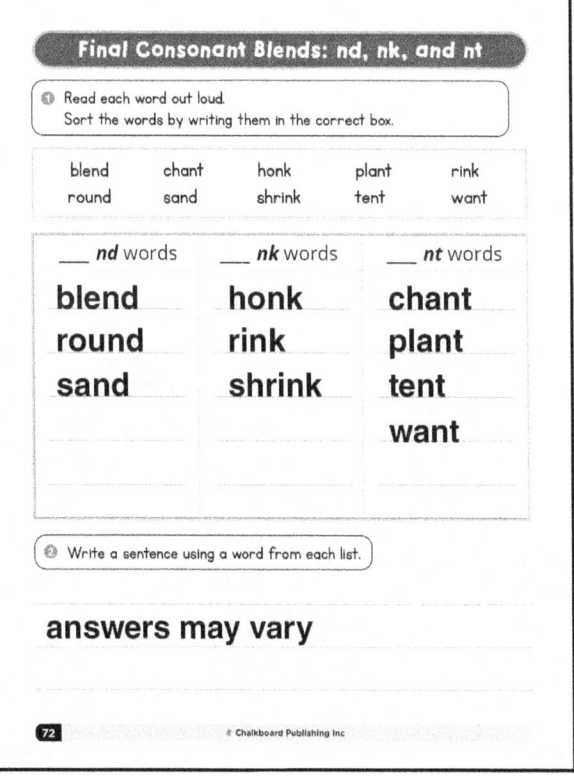

Answers

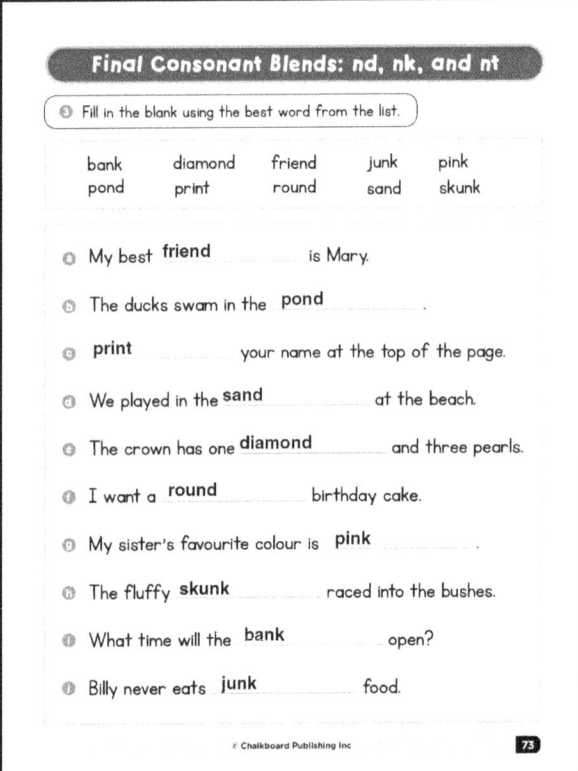

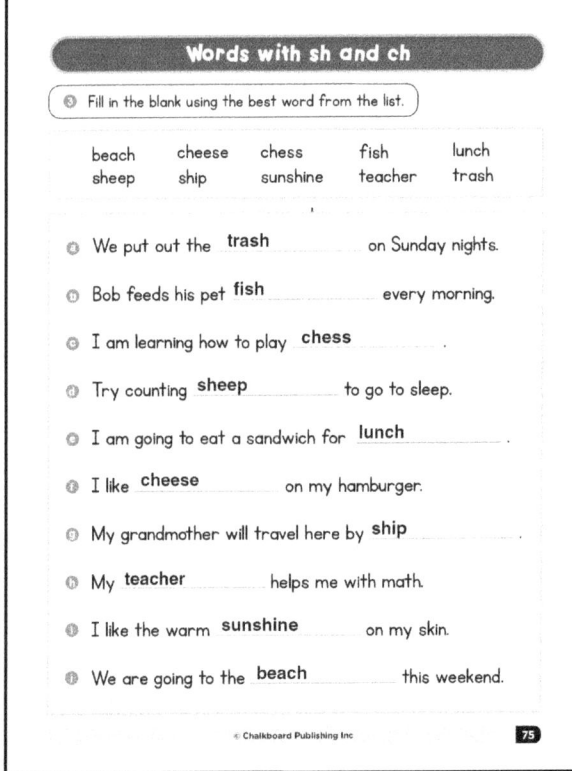

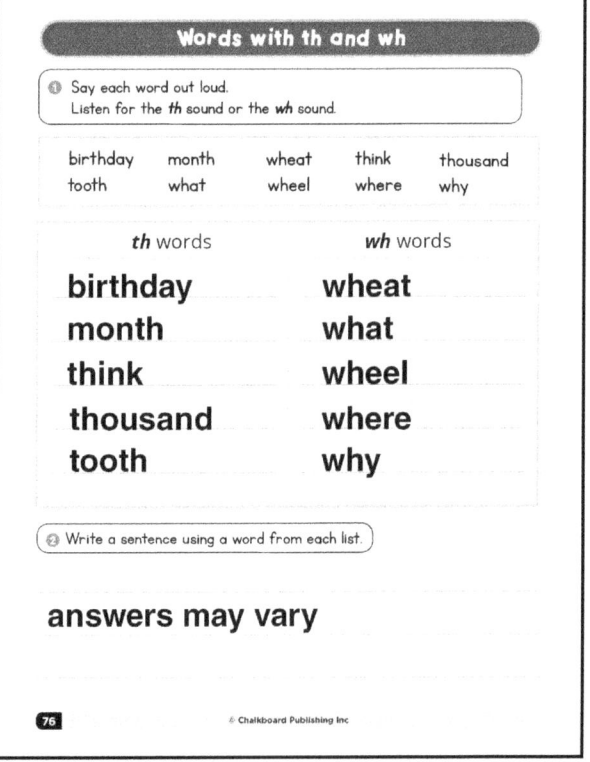

Answers

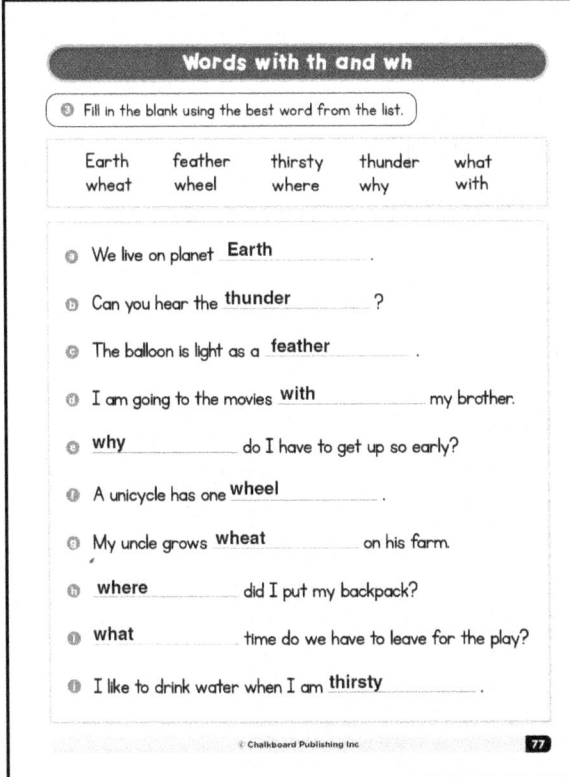

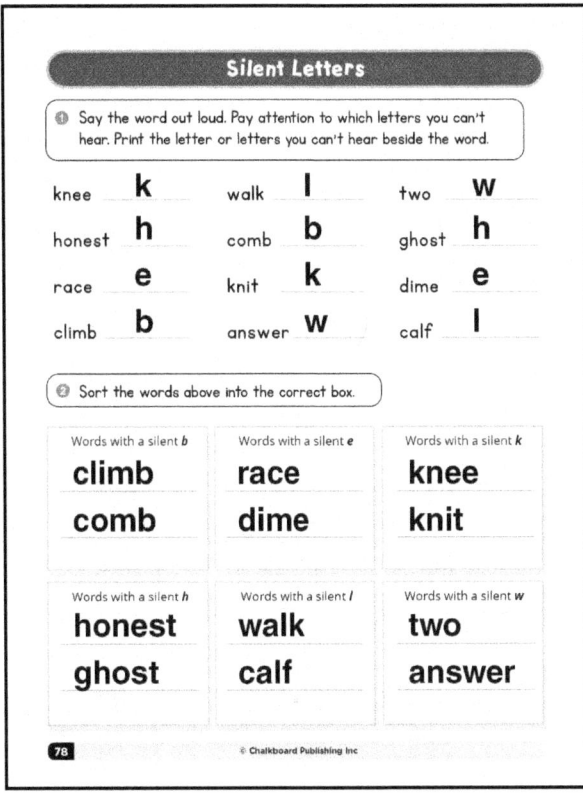

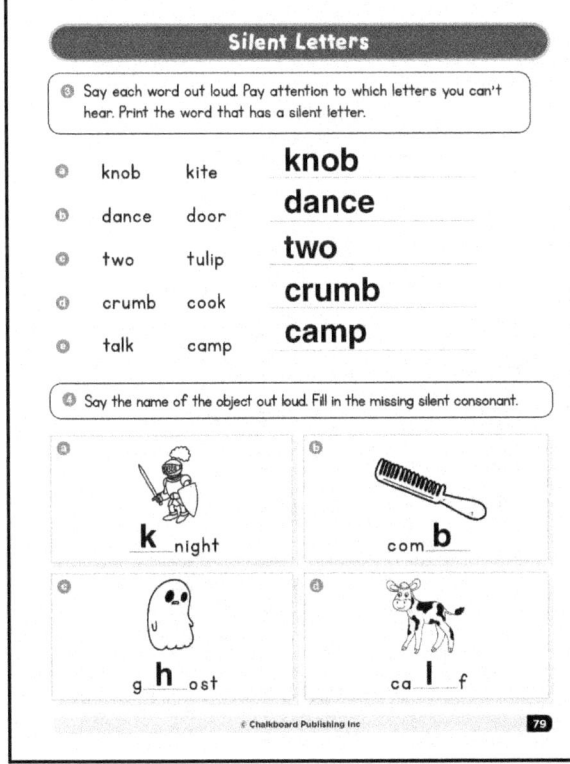

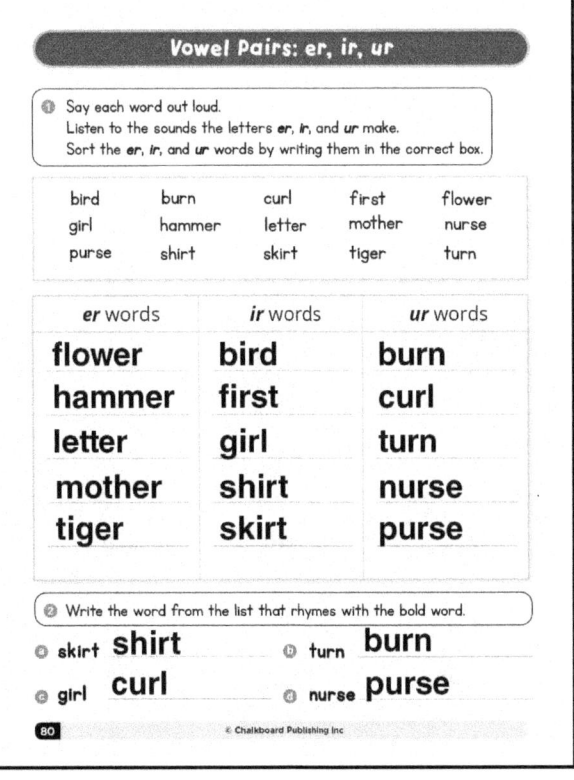

Answers

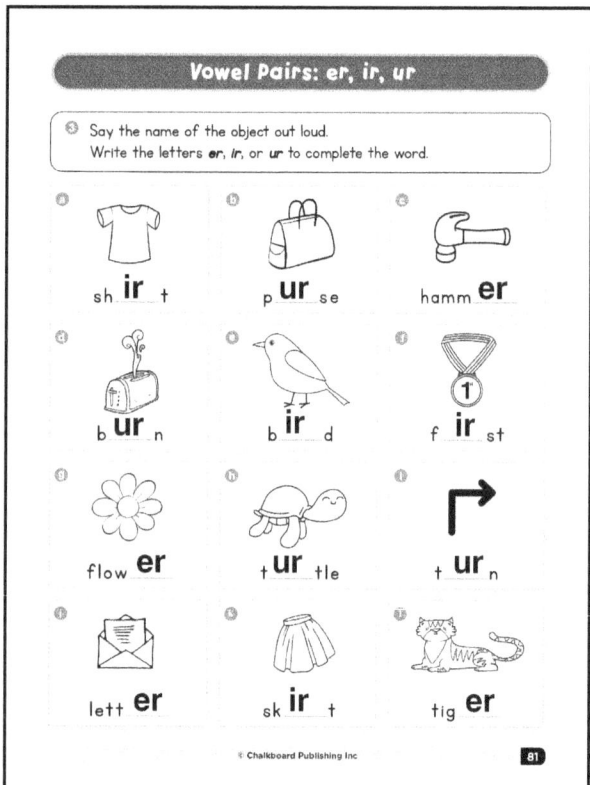

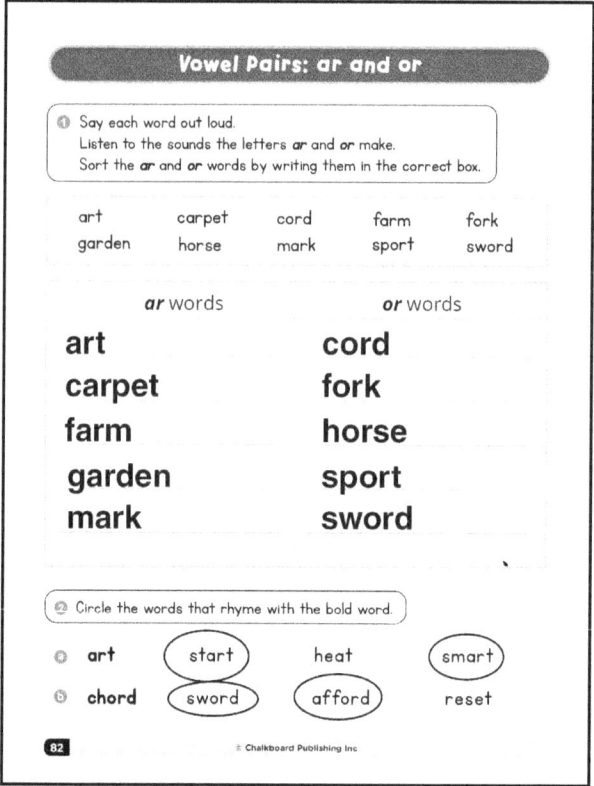

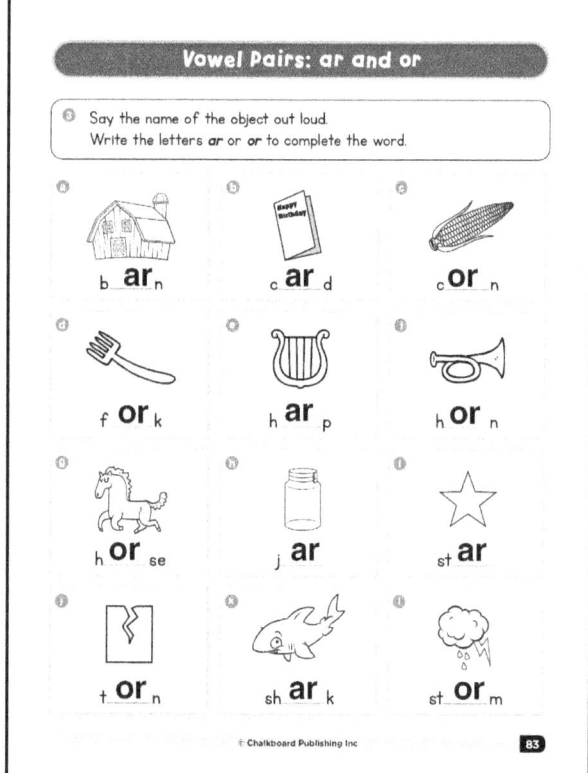

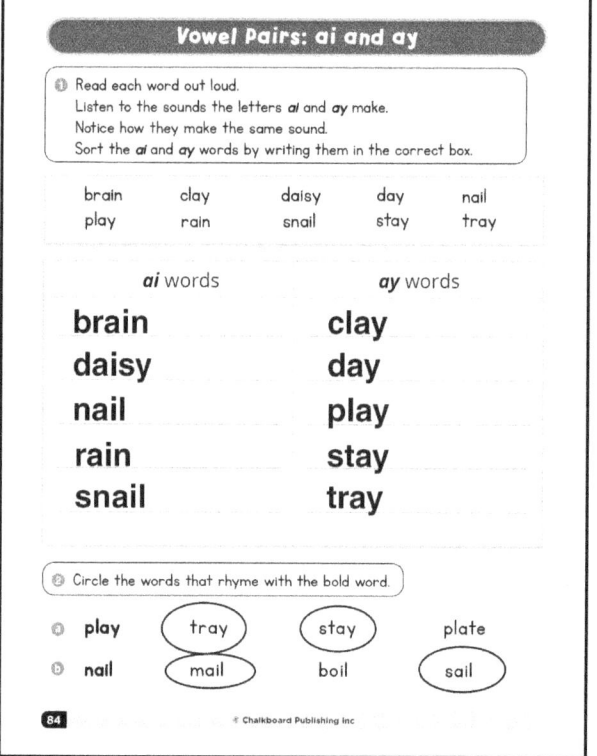

Answers

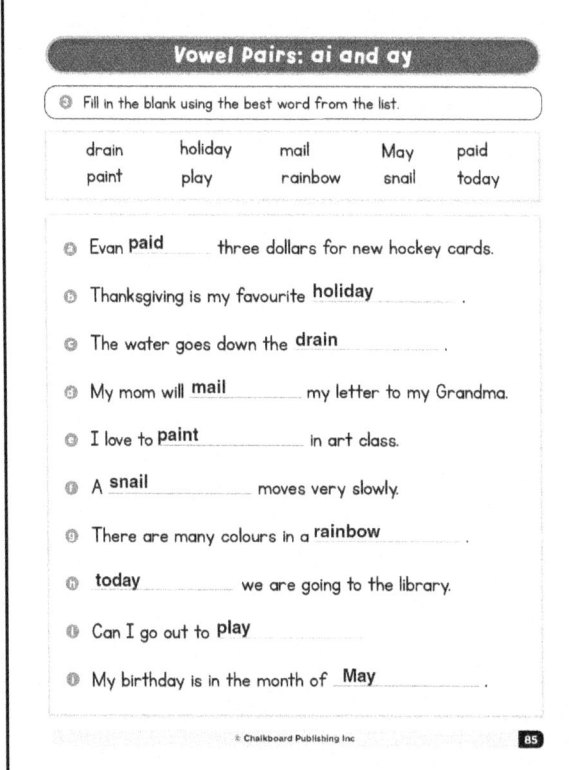

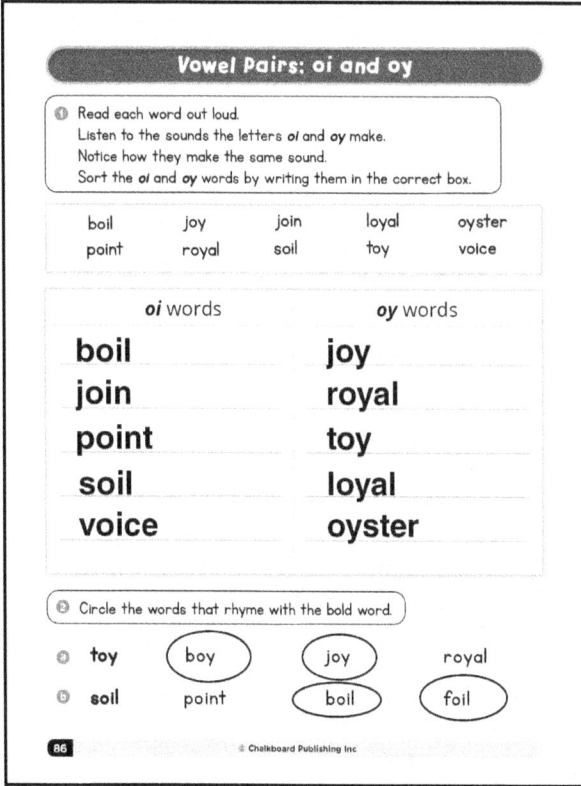

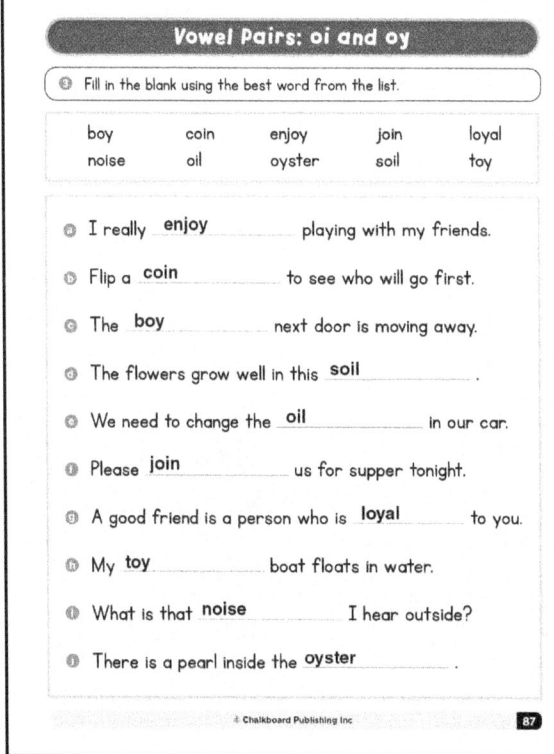

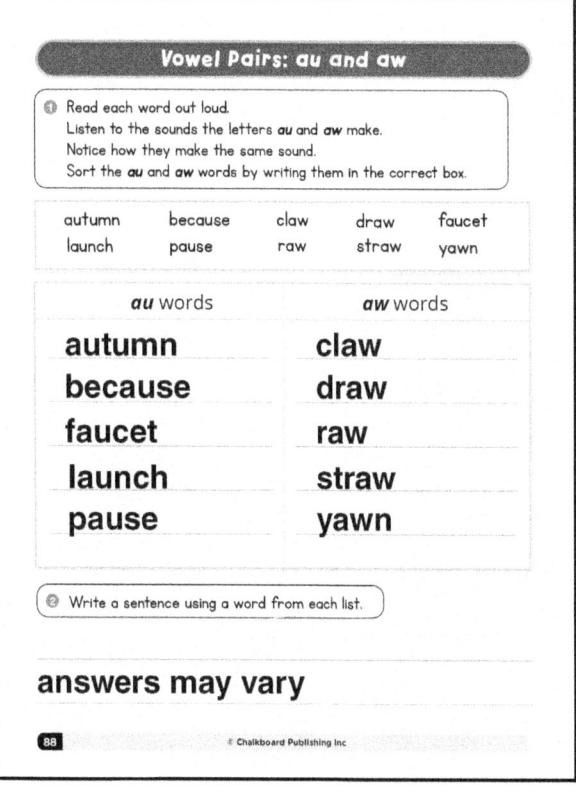

© Chalkboard Publishing Inc

Answers

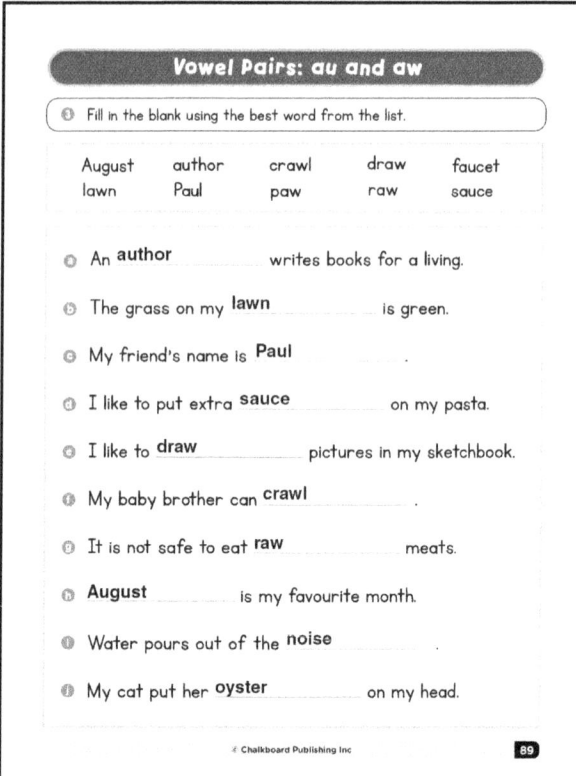

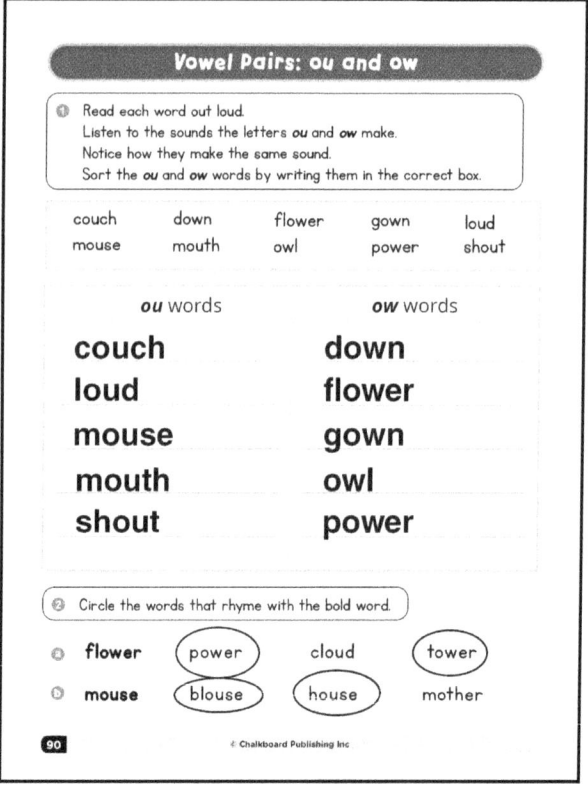

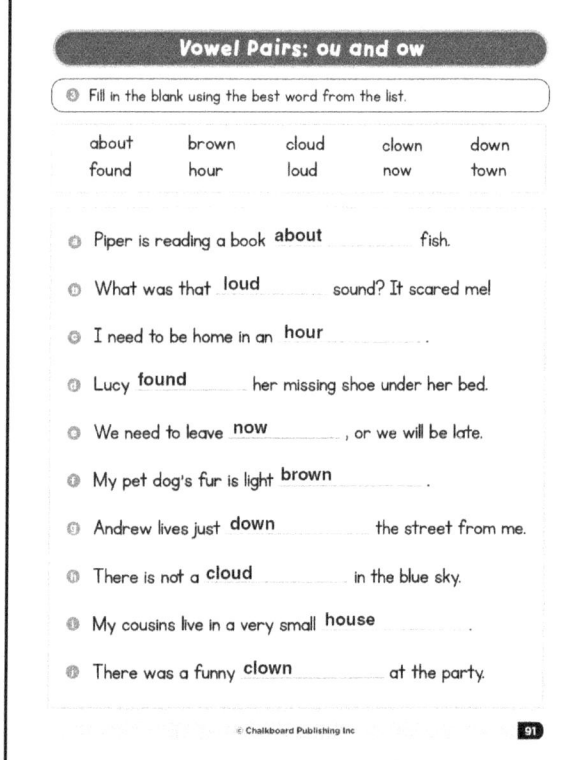

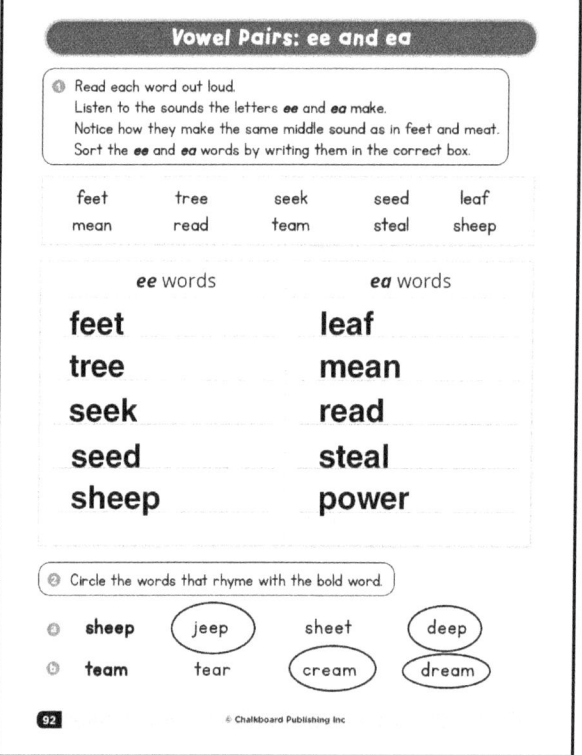

Answers

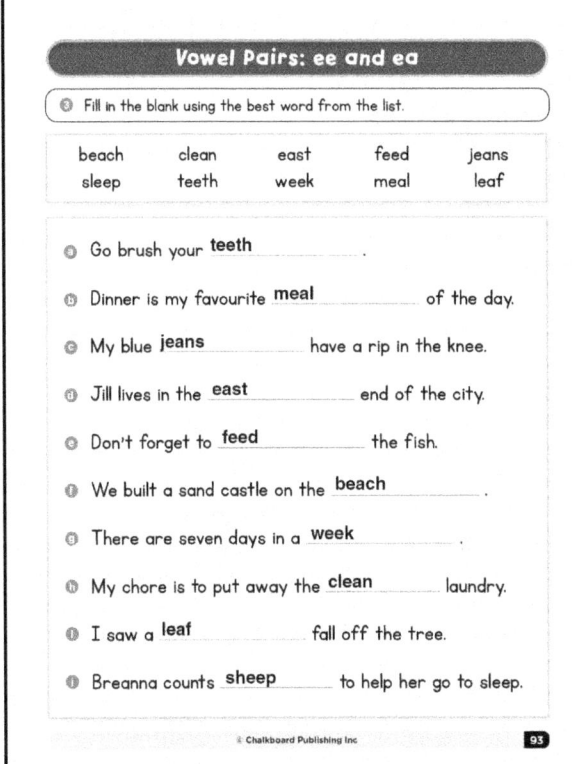

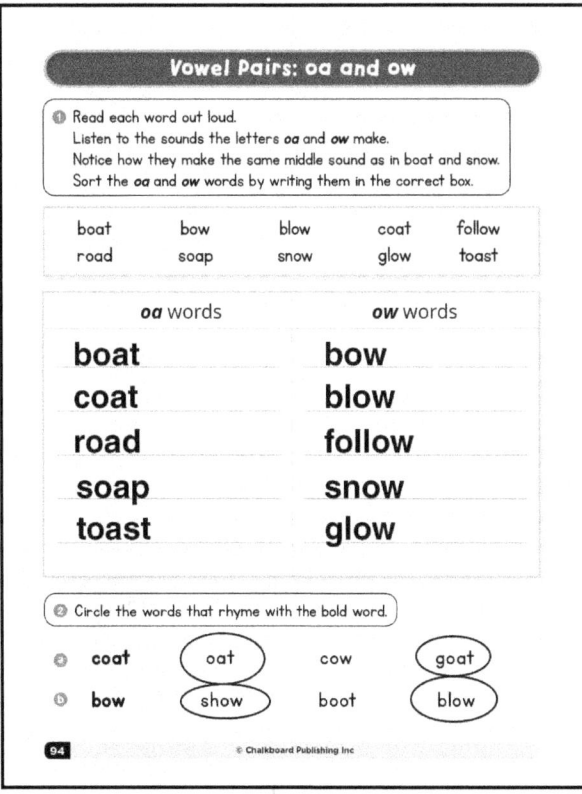

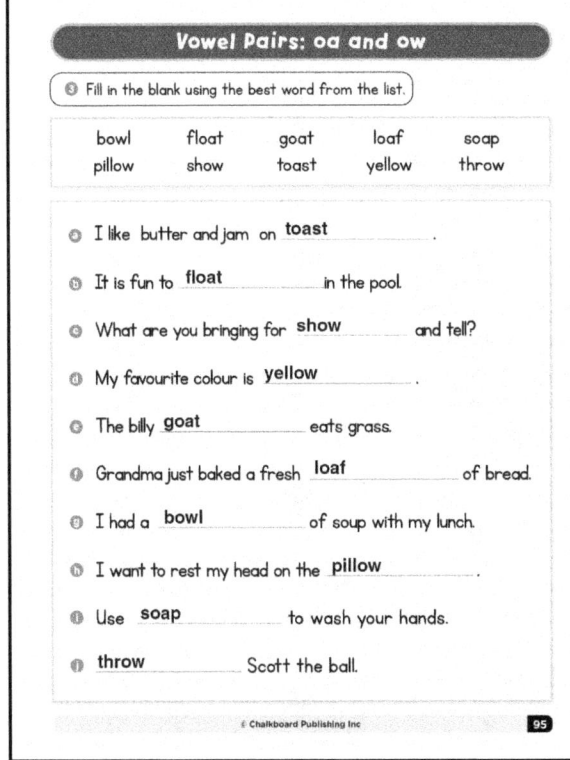

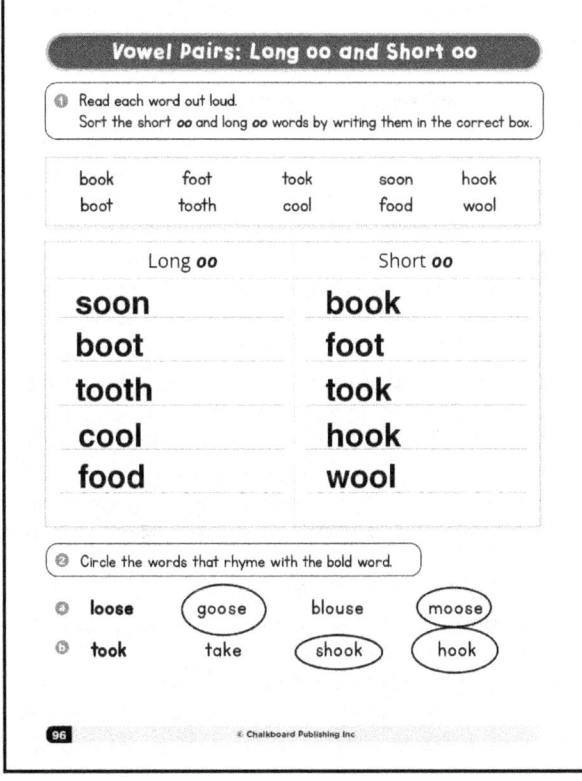

Answers

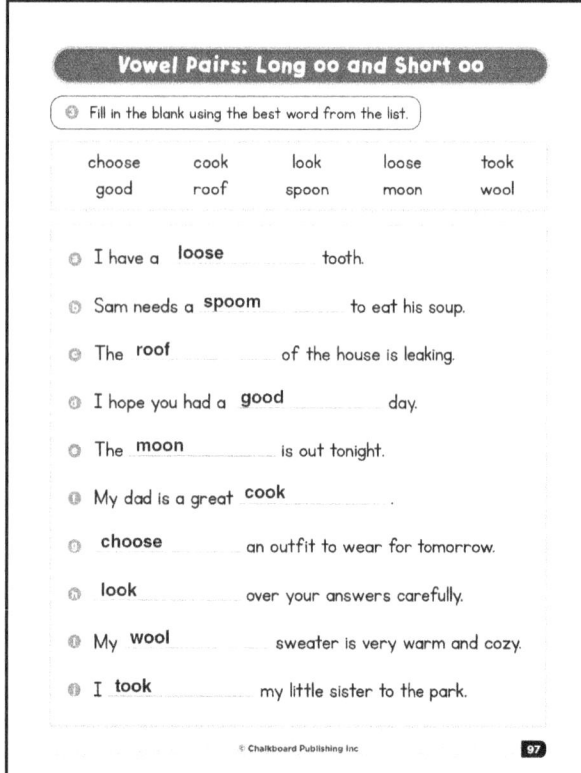

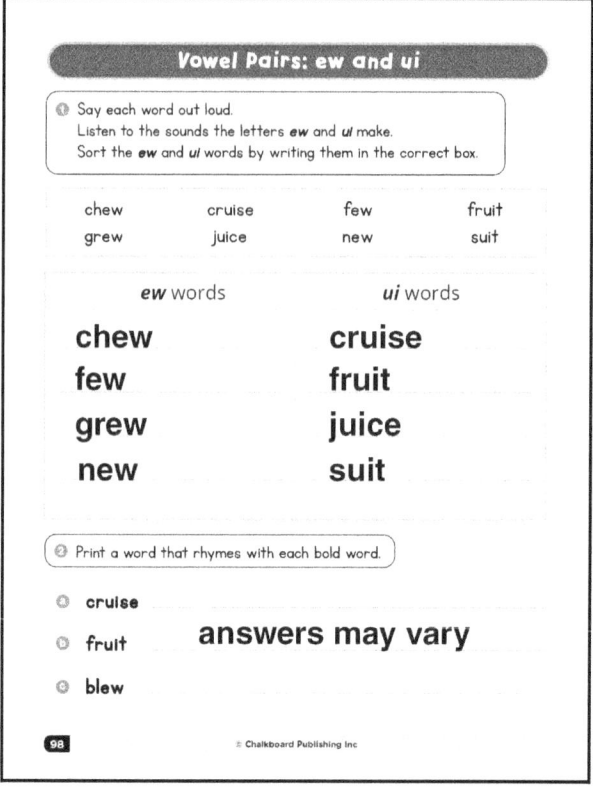

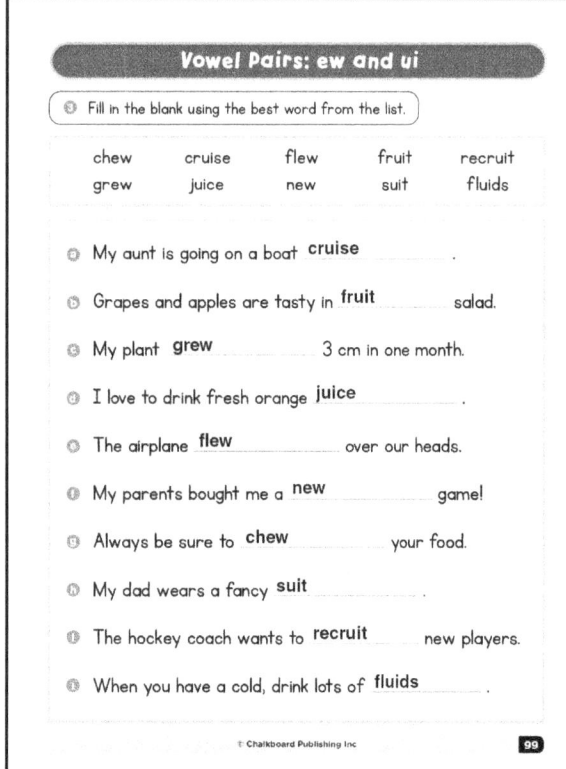

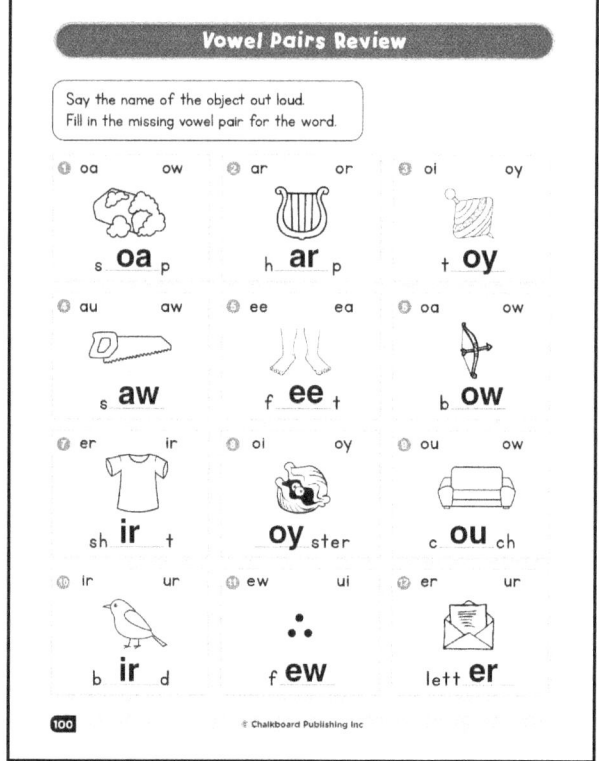

Answers

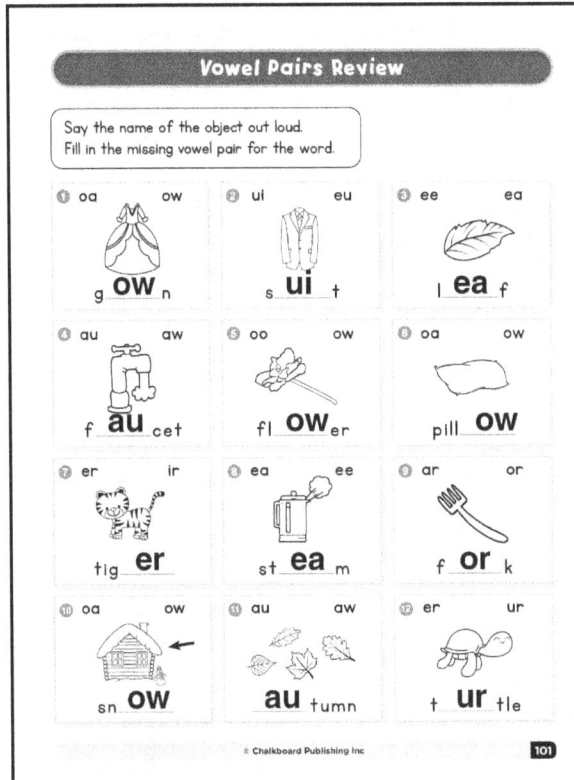

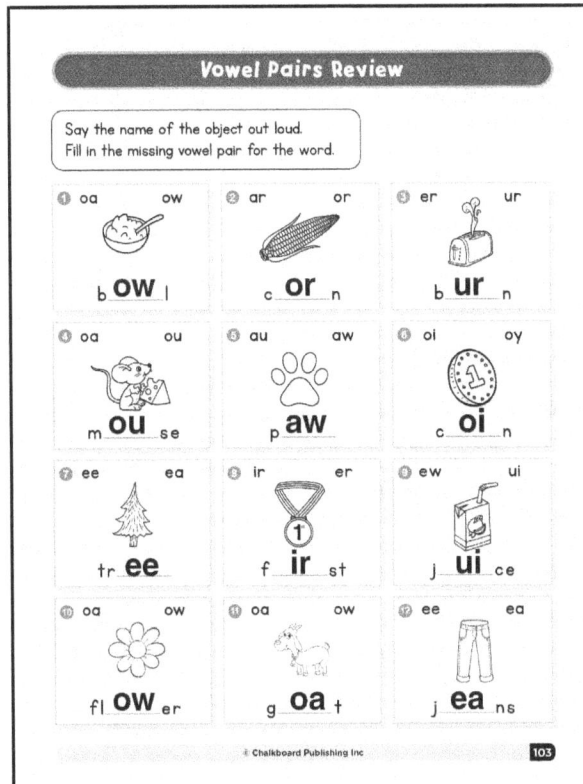

Congratulations!
Amazing Effort!

Phonics Expert!

- ⊘ **Beginning and Ending Letter Sounds**
- ⊘ **Short and Long Vowels**
- ⊘ **Consonant Blends**
- ⊘ **Final Consonant Blends**
- ⊘ **Silent Letters**
- ⊘ **Vowel Pairs**
- ⊘ **Word Families**